T0328076

The Modern Navajo Kitchen

The Modern Navajo Kitchen

Homestyle Recipes that Celebrate the Flavors and Traditions of the Diné

Diné bibee ó'ool'įįł bits'ą́ą́ dóó bóhoneedlį́įgo hooghan góne' ádaal'į́įgo daadánígíí

ALANA YAZZIE

wellfleet
press

Contents

Introduction

The Navajo, or Diné, are one of the largest Native American tribes in North America. We reside predominantly in the southwestern region of the United States. The Navajo Nation spans Arizona, New Mexico, and Utah and is one of the largest reservations in the US. The geographical landscapes differ across the Navajo Nation, and traditional food practices may vary based on the landscape. I grew up near the northern part, in Fruitland, New Mexico, near the San Juan River. It's quite common to farm and forage in the surrounding mountain landscapes. However, Navajos don't reside only on the Navajo Nation. We live across North America and even overseas, contributing to the urban Navajo culture that influences modern Navajo cuisine.

Navajo culture is rooted in traditional stories and practices that have been passed on through creation stories and songs. Likewise, the history of Navajo food is rich in diverse traditions that have been passed down from generation to generation.

A General Overview of Navajo Food History

Navajo food history is complex, and this is only a brief summary. Our food systems have been largely disrupted throughout history, and we are often relearning our traditional foods and practices. The Navajo people are innovative, resilient, and adaptive to changing environments.

Precolonization, Navajo people were seminomadic hunter-gatherers. We subsisted on small game like rabbits and prairie dogs, and foraged wild plants like wild spinach, wild onion, berries, and piñons (pine nuts). We lived off the land and what it naturally provided. We interacted with the surrounding Pueblo tribes and Spanish settlers when they arrived. It was around this time we learned farming practices and were introduced to sheep by the Pueblo and Spanish peoples. Sheep ended up becoming a large part of modern Navajo food culture, as the Navajos were resourceful in using all parts of the sheep, not only for food but also in traditional arts like Navajo rug weaving.

In the 1800s, Navajo food systems drastically changed due to war and the Long Walk (1864–1868). During the Long Walk, Navajos were forcibly removed by the United States government from their ancestral homelands and forced to walk to Bosque Redondo in eastern New Mexico. Many were killed or died along the way. Once they arrived, they were imprisoned and given meager food rations like bacon, flour, salt, sugar, lard, and coffee, all of which were uncommon to the Navajo diet. Although we were unfamiliar with these ingredients, we were resourceful and invented foods like fry bread, which is now a staple in modern Navajo cuisine. It was at this time that Americanized foods were integrated into our food system as a means of survival during these hard times.

From the late 1800s to early 1900s, Navajos still foraged for wild game and plants, but the practice became less prevalent with each generation. More of our land became settled, and we became more acquainted with reservation life once we were released after the Long Walk. Navajos became less seminomadic and began to farm corn, beans, squash, and melons, which were and are staples in the traditional Navajo diet. We learned from the surrounding tribes like the Hopi, Pueblo, and Apache. Mutton and lamb became staples in the Navajo diet as well as our culture, particularly from the Navajo-Churro sheep. For example, all parts of the sheep are used in making traditional foods like blood sausage, sheep head, and 'ach'ii' (wrapped intestines), and the wool is used to make rugs. (This cookbook does not include recipes like these, as sheep butchering could be a book of its own.)

Corn (blue, white, and yellow) is an integral part of Navajo food history. It is used not only for sustenance but also for our traditional Navajo ceremonies and practices. One of my favorite traditional Navajo ceremonies is the kinaaldá, a coming-of-age ceremony that celebrates Navajo womanhood and occurs when a Navajo girl experiences her first period. A timeless tradition that has carried on for generations, this big celebration takes place over four days and requires the help of family and community to offer teachings and blessings to the Navajo girl. One of the biggest parts of the ceremony is preparing a large (4 to 5 feet, or 1 m, in circumference) 'alkaad (Navajo Sweet Corn Cake, page 132) made of white cornmeal and raisins that is baked in the ground overnight. During this ceremony, the young Navajo woman is taught how to use traditional Navajo cooking tools, like grinding stones and stirring sticks, to prepare the cornmeal for the cake. Prayers and corn songs are shared, and offerings of cornmeal and pollen are made to the Diyin Diné'é (Holy People). I had a kinaaldá when I was younger, and the teachings and tools are a big part of who I am today.

In the mid-to-later parts of the 1900s, American foods became more incorporated into the Navajo diet, mainly due to US governmental efforts such as boarding schools, land and livestock reduction, commodity foods, and continued colonization. Young Navajo children were placed in boarding schools and were forced to assimilate to the American way of living. Despite these efforts by the US government, our elders continued to pass along their teachings, and so these traditions endured. It was around this time that traditional Navajo foods started to be reserved for special ceremonies and gatherings as more Navajos moved away from the Navajo Nation and fewer people farmed, hunted, and butchered their own meat.

Trading posts became staples in the Navajo community. Acting like local grocery stores, trading posts incorporated more American foods into our diets, including milk, eggs, SPAM (canned luncheon meat), canned fruits, and beef. Shimá (my mom) recalls shimásání (my maternal grandmother) coming back from the trading post with new food items she had never had before. The traders would have to share recipes on how to use these ingredients. New recipes were created, like the Potatoes and Ground Beef Bowl (page 97) and Navajo Tacos (page 93), as we navigated using these new-to-us food items. A lot of the foods supplied at the trading posts were shelf-stable, as most Navajo homes didn't have electricity—and some homes don't have access to electricity to this day.

Navajo Cuisine in the Twenty-First Century

In modern Navajo cuisine, trading posts still play a role in our food history as a place to purchase and buy American and traditional Navajo foods like flour, cornmeal, fresh mutton/lamb, and produce. You can also find traditional and modern Navajo cooking tools like grinding stones, stirring sticks, spotted enamelware kettles and cups, and cast-iron skillets. Over the decades, the traders have tailored their inventory to the local Navajo communities. Whenever I step into a trading post today, it feels like I have been transported back in time, and I often imagine shimásání doing her monthly shopping here.

Traditional Navajo foods like blue corn mush, kneel down bread, and Navajo tea are still part of our diets. However, a lot of these foods are made only at larger family gatherings and celebrations, like the Navajo Nation fairs and flea markets. There is more fusion of foods as we add in more flavors from surrounding communities, such as adding Hatch green chiles to roast mutton sandwiches. Flea markets, farmers' markets, roadside food stands, and Navajo-owned restaurants are important to modern Navajo cuisine. Since both traditional and modern Navajo foods can be found in these establishments, they bridge the gap between the past and the present.

In recent years there has been a movement toward Navajo food sovereignty and a push to revitalize traditional Navajo foods, cooking methods, and farming practices. A lot of traditional knowledge has been lost due to colonization, but as a community we are working to rebuild this knowledge. Like our ancestors, we are resilient! Much of this work has been shared through educating others and sharing cultural knowledge by the Navajo Nation government, traditional knowledge keepers, farmers, researchers, public health specialists, chefs, and food enthusiasts like me.

Among the younger generations, there has been great interest in growing Navajo crops like Navajo corn, pumpkins, and squash. Organizations like Native Seeds Search have Native Access programs, where Native farmers and gardeners can access heirloom seeds that are being revitalized in their local communities. In turn, this access allows Navajos to start or revitalize home gardens in their backyards.

Cove, Arizona

Workshops and classes offered to local communities teach individuals how to prepare traditional recipes, like kneel down bread and blue corn mush. Navajo researchers have also done more investigation into our cooking methods, like using juniper ash, which is high in nutrients (especially calcium), in our cornmeal recipes. This knowledge has empowered our communities to relearn these traditional recipes and incorporate these foods back into our modern diets.

The internet and social media have also played a huge role in revitalizing our Navajo foodways, like the ones I share on my food blog, *The Fancy Navajo*. Online communities have come together to share traditional knowledge, classic recipes, and modern fusions, bolstered by online workshops, podcasts, and lectures. These online resources are especially important for those of us who have moved away from the Navajo Nation.

My Personal History with Navajo Cuisine

Before we begin, I would like to share my Navajo clans. My maternal clan is Tot'sohn'nii (Big Water Clan) and my paternal clan is Ta'neeszahnii (Tangle Clan). My maternal grandfather's clan is Tábaaha (Waters Edge Clan) and my paternal grandfather's clan is Kinyaa'áanii (Towering House Clan). These are the clans that identify me as Diné woman. If we are related, then you will have to let me know.

I have always had a deep love and appreciation for food. Living in northwestern New Mexico, I grew up not only with southwestern and New Mexican cuisines, but also a variety of Native American cuisines. My teachers were shik'éí (my family), and cooking brought our family together. From shimá I learned how to be patient in the kitchen as she taught me how to cook from scratch. Shizhe'é (my dad) taught me the importance of eating healthily and having a balanced diet. Shínaaí (my older brother) taught me how to bake and encouraged me to always try new foods. From shimásání I learned to be independent, as she took care of her flock of sheep every day, all while living with no running water or electricity. These teachings laid the foundation for my love of food and cooking, and they're what I want to pass along to shich'é'é (my daughter).

At an early age, I always wanted to be in the kitchen with shimá, and one of the first things I wanted to make was náneeskaadí (flour tortillas , also called Navajo tortillas in this book). I was always intrigued by how my mom never used any measuring cups or spoons, only the cups of her hands. A scoop of this and a pinch of that. It was like a magic trick that I didn't quite understand when I tried replicating it on my own. My tortillas would never turn out exactly like hers, but she always encouraged me to keep trying.

When I was in my preteens, we had a traditional healer come over for dinner, but my mom had to stay at work longer than planned. Our guest arrived before she did, so I took it upon myself to make náneeskaadí for the mutton stew she had put in the slow cooker earlier that day. It was one of the first times I had ever cooked for someone other than my immediate family. But I wanted to surprise my mom by showing her that I could make bread like her. So, into the kitchen

I went, replicating her tortilla magic. My tortillas weren't perfectly shaped like hers, but they tasted delicious! I remember being nervous as I served the bread to our guest. The first thing he said was "Ayoo' shił łikan!" which translates to "It tastes really good to me!" in Navajo.

After graduating college and settling into my adult life in Phoenix, Arizona, I found comfort in learning how to make my favorite childhood meals. Although I had learned to make some Navajo dishes growing up, I began to realize I didn't know much about traditional Navajo foods like juniper ash, dried steam corn, and sumac berry. So, each time I went home, I made it a priority to learn a new Navajo recipe. I was still not understanding my mom's magic tricks of using no measurements, so she encouraged me to write down the recipes, and soon I became confident in making things like blue corn mush and steam corn stew.

In 2014, I created my blog, *The Fancy Navajo*, which documents my life as a contemporary Diné woman living in the city. It began as my creative outlet to explore my Navajo heritage through my own lens. I showcased and photographed contemporary Navajo life, from fashion to food, in a happy and vibrant way that I hadn't seen in mainstream media before. Even though I no longer lived at home, I wanted to inspire others to embrace their culture, wherever they live. It quickly became a resource for anyone who wanted to learn about Navajo culture and food. Most importantly, my blog served as a resource for other Navajos who may have not learned how to make traditional recipes.

Later, I began to experiment with ingredients like blue cornmeal and ground sumac berries, coming up with new ways of using them. When I was growing up, a lot of traditional Navajo ingredients were reserved for large family gatherings or traditional ceremonies. I began to wonder what the future of Navajo cuisine would look like. How could I adapt these traditional ingredients into my current lifestyle and revitalize them? So, I began incorporating them into recipes that became blue corn quiche and Navajo boba milk tea. My contemporary Navajo recipes (or Fancy Navajo recipes, as I like to call them), like blue corn cupcakes and blue corn cookies, are some of the most popular on my blog.

How to Use This Book

This cookbook is a celebration of my Diné heritage and my love of food. I've included a variety of recipes, from traditional Navajo dishes like Steam Corn Stew (page 73), Blue Corn Mush Breakfast Fruit Bowl (page 49), and Savory Blue Corn Mush Bowl (page 83) to more modern recipes like Navajo Tacos (page 93). I've also included modern fusions, like Piñon Lattes (page 158) and Blue Corn Strawberry Shortcakes (page 140). These are homestyle recipes that can easily be incorporated into your weekly meal plans. I make the recipes featured in the breads section on a weekly basis. But it's important to remember that as you learn to make Náneeskaadí (page 33), for example, it may take a few times to master it. So don't worry if your tortillas don't look perfect the first time you make them. As long as they taste "ayoo łikan!", just have fun and keep trying.

What you'll learn from this cookbook is that modern Navajo cuisine is simple yet full of flavor. The Navajo are resourceful and inventive in our cooking methods and how we use our traditional ingredients. A lot of the recipes come from foods that we have grown over centuries. These recipes also stem from resiliency and perseverance. Postcolonization, our diets started to contain more processed foods. Yet throughout all of this, Navajo people have preserved and have started to reclaim our Indigenous foodways by incorporating both modern and traditional cuisines.

This cookbook is a stepping stone to learning about Navajo foods and is not all-encompassing. I encourage you to learn more about Navajo foodways. If you are Navajo, I encourage you to learn about your family traditions. Talk with your elders and don't be afraid to write down the recipes. Experiment with the recipes in this cookbook and make them your own. Add your own personal touches and get creative. Most importantly, have fun and enjoy the delicious food. I hope you enjoy cooking and eating these recipes as much as I do!

The Navajo Pantry

The modern Navajo pantry includes a variety of grains, dried and canned goods, fresh meats, vegetables, and spices that you may already have on hand. Most of the ingredients and tools can be found at your local grocery store. There are a few ingredients that are regional and seasonal to the Southwest and the Navajo Nation. For this reason, I've included a list of Native-owned businesses that sell some of these items online (see page 164). Some of the pantry staples in the list below can be substituted for other ingredients, and I have included these substitutions where applicable.

Tools & Equipment

You won't need too many extra tools and equipment when it comes to Navajo cooking, as most of these recipes are meant to be made in a typical home kitchen. However, there are a few items that may not be common that you may need.

Round cast-iron skillet or pan (8 inches, or 20 cm): This skillet is commonly used for making fry bread (page 34) and grilling meats. Since this pan is used to deep-fry, you will want to make sure it is at least 1½ inches (4 to 5 cm) deep.

Round cast-iron griddle, comal, or crepe pan (9½ inches, or 24 cm): A round cast-iron griddle is traditionally used to make Navajo Tortillas (page 33) and Blue Corn Pancakes (page 61). I personally use a nonstick crepe pan, as I find it's easier to clean. The size of the pan can range from 8 to 10 inches (20 to 25 cm).

Rolling pin: A rolling pin will be needed to help roll out dough for breads like Navajo Tortillas (page 33), noodles for Dumpling Stew (page 70), and desserts like White Corn Scones with Apricots (page 65). You won't find a rolling pin in a traditional Navajo pantry, as most of these recipes are made by stretching out the dough with your hands; however, I recommend using a rolling pin for beginners to modern Navajo cuisine.

Fine-mesh strainer: This tool will be used to sift, strain, and combine ingredients. I like to have a large, medium, and small fine-mesh strainer on hand.

Kitchen torch: A kitchen torch will be needed to make juniper ash (see page 23). Because you'll be igniting tree sprigs, use a powerful propane kitchen torch.

Campfire grill: A campfire grill at least 16 by 16 inches (41 by 41 cm) or larger will be needed when making juniper ash (see page 23). You can also use the campfire grill to make Navajo Tortillas (page 33) and Blue Corn Patties (page 38).

Candy thermometer: A candy thermometer will be needed to make Sumac Berry Jam (page 119).

8-inch (20 cm) square baking dish: You will need an 8-inch (20 cm) square pan to make Navajo Sweet Corn Cake (page 132).

9-inch (23 cm) square baking dish: You will need a 9-inch (23 cm) square pan to make Braised Red Chile Mutton Stew (page 80) and Chili Bean Cornmeal Casserole (page 106).

Whisk: Traditionally, Navajo wooden stirring sticks are used in Navajo cooking. A metal whisk can be used if you don't have one. I like to have a regular-size whisk and a smaller whisk.

Blender or food processer: This tool is needed to make chile sauces, syrups, and Piñon Nut Butter (page 120). I prefer to use a blender for sauces and syrups, and a food processor for the piñon butter.

Coffee grinder: This tool is needed to grind corn for Navajo Coffee/Corn Creamer (page 161). If you have a traditional Navajo grinding stone, you can use that instead.

Ice pop molds: A six-slot ice pop mold will be needed to make Sumac and Strawberry Greek Yogurt Ice Pops (page 143).

7- to 10-quart (6 to 9 L) slow cooker: The slow cooker is needed to make soups and stews like Chili Beans (page 74) and Steam Corn Stew (page 73).

15½-quart (15 L) tamale steamer: Use a tamale steamer to make Navajo Tamales (page 100). You may also use a stockpot with a steamer basket in lieu of a tamale steamer.

Mainstays of the Navajo Pantry

The mainstays of the Navajo pantry are simple, yet the flavors they add make Navajo cuisine unique. Some of these items may not be found in your local grocery store. Where possible, I have included substitutions. You can refer to the list of Native American businesses that sell these items online on page 164.

Roasted Cornmeal (Blue, Yellow, and White)
Cornmeal is a staple in Navajo cuisine. A special variety of Navajo corn is used to make roasted stone-ground cornmeal, which is less sweet than common grocery store cornmeal and more finely ground. However, as long as the cornmeal is stone-ground,

any variety can be used. If you cannot find roasted cornmeal, you can roast your own at home (page 27).

I often get asked if masa harina can be used instead of roasted cornmeal. Masa harina is treated with lime, making the flavor slightly different, so I don't recommend it. Roasted cornmeal can be found at local flea markets and trading posts on the Navajo Nation. It may also be sold at specialty grocery stores or purchased online.

Ground Sumac Berries

The Navajo variety of sumac is three-leaf sumac (*Rhus trilobata* Nutt.), which is common to the Southwest. Ground sumac berries are different from the ground sumac that may be found in grocery stores and Mediterranean markets. It has a similar flavor and can be used, but I don't recommend it, because salt is sometimes added. The colors and taste are also less vibrant than those of the three-leaf sumac. This variety of ground sumac berries can be found at local flea markets and trading posts on the Navajo Nation. Sometimes you may also be able to find it online.

Navajo Tea

Navajo tea is an Indigenous wild tea that is commonly called greenthread tea. It is typically harvested during the summer months in the Southwest. Navajo tea is sold in a preassembled bundle and can be found at local flea markets, trading posts on the Navajo reservation, and sometimes online.

Dried Steam Corn (Neeshjį́zhii')

Neeshjį́zhii' is freshly harvested Navajo white corn that has been steamed in a fire pit and then dried. Steam corn has an earthy, roasted corn flavor. Dried steam corn is usually made during the fall season and can be purchased at local flea markets and trading posts on the Navajo Nation. Navajo farmers also sell it online.

Fresh Corn

Fresh corn is a staple in Navajo cuisine but is only available during the fall harvest. It is usually dried and saved for later. The fresh corn used is a special variety of Navajo corn (dent corn), which is less sweet than common grocery store corn. The only recipe that absolutely requires fresh Navajo corn is Kneel Down Bread (page 42). Unless noted in the recipe, fresh sweet corn sold at local farmers' markets or grocery stores can be used instead.

Dried Corn Husks

Traditional corn dishes are made with dried corn husks. These are used as natural baking liners. Dried corn husks can be found at most local grocery stores or at trading posts on the Navajo Nation.

Squash and Pumpkins

Navajo varieties of squash and pumpkin are typically used in Navajo cooking. Navajo farmers sell these along the roadside, at farmers' markets, or at flea markets during the fall harvest on the Navajo Nation. Squash and pumpkins can also be found at your local farmers' market or grocery store.

Potatoes

Russet or Idaho potatoes are commonly used in Navajo cooking.

Alliums

Traditionally, wild Navajo onions were foraged and can still be found on the Navajo Nation. However, green onion, white onions, yellow onion, red onions, and garlic found at local farmers' markets and grocery stores can be used.

Flour

All-purpose flour is commonly used in modern Navajo cuisine. Typically, Blue Bird Flour, sold by the Cortez Milling Company, is a beloved favorite among the Navajos. However, this flour is bleached. I recommend using the unbleached version, Red Rose Flour, or any type of unbleached all-purpose flour from brands such as King Arthur Baking Company or Bob's Red Mill.

Baking Powder and Salt

Navajo cuisine includes a lot of bread and baked goods that require baking powder and salt. These are must-have staples when cooking.

Beans

Pinto beans are the most commonly used in Navajo cuisine, and dried pinto beans are a staple in Navajo pantries. Canned pinto beans are less common but can be substituted. I recommend rinsing canned beans before using them as they may have added salt.

Piñons (Pine Nuts)

Piñons, or pine nuts, are common in the Navajo pantry. Piñons are a once-a-year treat during harvesting season in the late summer and fall. They are usually roasted. They are commonly sold at local flea markets and trading posts on the Navajo Nation.

Alternatively, raw pine nuts from the local grocery store can be substituted.

Fresh Fruit

Fresh fruit such as strawberries, blueberries, raspberries, bananas, grapes, melons, peaches, apricots, cherries, and oranges are commonly added to Blue Corn Mush Breakfast Fruit Bowls (page 49), desserts like Blue Corn Strawberry Shortcakes (page 140), and drinks like Strawberry Navajo Iced Tea (page 150). Depending on the season, fresh fruits change throughout the year.

Dried Fruit and Jam

Dried fruit is common in the Navajo pantry as it is used to sweeten traditional Navajo desserts like Navajo Sweet Corn Cake (page 132). When I was growing up, raisins and prunes were the most common. I like using dried cranberries in place of raisins, as they're less sweet. Apricots and peaches are also dried for use in recipes like White Corn Scones with Apricots (page 65).

Chiles

Several varieties of chile peppers are common in Navajo cooking, including:

Roasted New Mexico Hatch green chiles: Green chiles are harvested and roasted in the fall. Then the roasted chiles are frozen and used throughout the year (page 25) in soups/stews and sandwiches.

Dried New Mexico Hatch red chiles: These peppers are used to make red chile sauces for tamales and stews.

Fresh jalapeños/serrano peppers: Contemporary Navajos like spicy foods. Jalapeños and serrano peppers are served with savory meals to add extra spice.

SPAM/Canned Luncheon Meat

SPAM, or canned luncheon meat, is a shelf-stable meat that is a beloved favorite. It can be used in place of fresh meat and is served in burritos and soups.

Fresh Meats

Mutton and lamb are used interchangeably in Navajo cuisine depending on personal preference. Navajo churro sheep meat is traditionally used in dishes like Braised Red Chile Mutton Stew (page 80), Steam Corn Stew (page 73), and Lamb Sandwiches (page 90). In modern times, US mutton and lamb are also commonly used. Mutton and lamb can be purchased at local butchers, trading posts, and grocery stores on and near the Navajo reservation. Beef can be substituted for any of the recipes that call for mutton or lamb.

Ground beef is also a staple in modern Navajo cuisine. Unless noted, 80 percent lean/20 percent fat is commonly used, but any fat percentage can be used based on your liking.

Fats and Oils

Shortening and lard are traditionally used in Navajo cooking, especially when making fry bread. When I was growing up, my family used vegetable and canola oil instead. Similarly, olive oil and butter were used for frying and baking. For the recipes in this book, you will need extra-virgin olive oil.

Sheep and Their Place in Navajo Cuisine

Sheep are important in Navajo food culture as they are one of the main sources of meat used in Navajo cooking. Navajos are well known for their sheep herding and butchering and both are coveted traditional skills. Shimásání was a sheepherder and butcher. She tended to her more than thirty-five sheep and fifteen head of cattle every day in Steamboat, Arizona (and my great-grandma had over one hundred sheep!). Shimásání tended the sheep alone with some help from relatives in the surrounding area when she needed it, but she did this all with no running water and electricity. My siblings and I spent summers with her and she taught us how to tend the sheep with her. I always enjoyed when the lambs were born. Most animals aren't allowed inside Navajo homes, but during the colder months the lambs and baby goats were allowed to stay inside with my grandma. She would let us feed the baby animals with milk bottles.

The best meals were always made at my grandma's house. When there was a special family gathering or celebration, shimásání would invite everyone over to butcher a sheep. I was always impressed how she did this so effortlessly as she guided the family in the processing of the sheep. Shimásání only went to school until the fifth grade, but she knew every part of the sheep as she easily maneuvered her knife around the sheep organs like an expert surgeon. Some helped to prepare the sheep, from tending the fire to cutting, slicing, and cleaning the meat. Others helped prepare the sides for the feast like stews, salads, blue corn mush, and tortillas or fry bread. One of the most tedious tasks was to clean and prepare the sheep intestines that would then be wrapped around the sheep fat to make 'ach'ii'. Someone else might have been preparing blood sausage, which uses the sheep's stomach as a casing to be filled with the sheep's blood combined with potatoes and blue cornmeal. All these foods were cooked over an open fire and when everything was finished, it was the BEST meal ever!

Sheepherding and butchering are a big part of my culture; however, it is not something that is frequently practiced by the average Navajo family in the twenty-first century. In modern times, we rely on butchers, trading posts, grocery stores, flea markets, and Navajo restaurants to provide mutton and lamb meat. One of my first stops when I go back to the Navajo Nation is to stop at the flea market for roast mutton in dishes like Lamb Sandwiches (page 90) and Traditional Mutton Ribs (page 89). I commonly stock up on mutton or lamb stew meat and freeze it for later use for recipes like Steam Corn Stew (page 73), Dumpling Stew (page 70), Mutton and Vegetable Stew (page 69), and Braised Red Chile Mutton Stew (page 80). Navajos have also adapted our diets to other meats like beef, chicken, pork, and seafood, or have chosen to be vegetarian or vegan, eschewing meat altogether.

Sheep butchering is typically reserved for large family gatherings, ceremonies, and special events. One of the most unique features of sheep butchering is that all parts of the sheep are utilized. The sheep skin and wool are used to make rugs, thread, drinking vessels, or turned into yarn to make rugs. The meat is prepared in a variety of ways from boiling and frying to grilling and roasting. I've broken the list into most commonly eaten and less common/traditional delicacies. The most commonly eaten parts are typically easier to find at a local butcher, but the less common parts are typically eaten when a sheep is freshly butchered. Please note that depending on each family, this list may be slightly different.

Most Commonly Eaten

* **Backbone:** Used for making stews and soups.

* **Legs:** Used for making stews, soups, and roast mutton.

* **Arms:** Used for making stews, soups, and roast mutton.

* **Ribs:** Usually roasted and eaten as is.

* **Liver:** Usually roasted and eaten as is.

* **Fat:** Roasted and eaten as is, or used in 'ach'ii'-making.

Less Common or Traditional Delicacies

* **Stomach:** Used as the casing to make blood sausage.

* **Intestines:** Used to make 'ach'ii'.

* **Blood:** Used to make blood sausage.

* **Colon:** Used to make 'ach'ii'.

* **Heart:** Usually roasted and eaten as is.

* **Head (including the eyes, tongue, and ears):** Usually roasted and eaten as is.

* **Lungs:** Usually roasted and eaten as is.

* **Kidneys:** Usually roasted and eaten as is.

Beyond the Basics: Culinary Ash and Roasting Techniques

In this section you will learn how to elevate simple ingredients to make your Navajo recipes even more delicious.

How to Make Juniper Ash
Gad bee łeeshch'iih

The juniper tree is common in the Southwest, and juniper ash, or gad bee łeeshch'iih in Navajo, is a staple in the Navajo pantry. However, it is not something you can buy at your local grocery store. It is typically made at home or purchased from Navajo food purveyors on the Navajo Nation. Traditionally, it is made outside in large batches over an open fire, and the ashes are stored for use throughout the year. Since the juniper branches are usually wild-foraged in isolated areas, avoid selecting branches in high-traffic areas because they may have been treated with pesticides or other unknown chemicals. A common Navajo teaching is to "take only what you need," so be mindful when foraging juniper branches.

Juniper ash is often used when cooking with blue cornmeal. I like to call juniper ash a Navajo superfood. The juniper ash helps break down the cornmeal to make it more digestible, and it infuses the cornmeal with nutrients like zinc, iron, and magnesium. Most importantly, it provides a source of calcium. The ash also deepens the blue color of blue cornmeal. If you cook without it, then the color of the blue cornmeal will be more of a purplish blue. (It is also called Navajo baking powder because when dissolved it acts like an alkaline solution.) Juniper ash can also be found at local flea markets, trading posts on the Navajo reservation, and sometimes online. Please note that the juniper ash used in the recipes in this book can be omitted, but just be aware that the colors and flavors may be slightly off as a result.

SAFETY NOTE: This is a modern approach to making a small batch of juniper ash. Take the necessary precautions to ensure this is done safely. Juniper ash must be created outside and away from anything that could catch fire, as there will be open flames and smoke. I do this in my backyard at least 15 feet (5 m) away from my house on ground that has gravel. Avoid making juniper ash on windy days.

Yield: ½ cup (225 g)
Prep time: 10 minutes
Cook time: 20 minutes

4 or 5 juniper branches (12 inches, or 30 cm, long) or about 12 ounces (340 g) juniper tree sprigs with berries removed

EQUIPMENT

Sheet pan

Aluminum foil

Campfire grill

Kitchen torch

Medium sifter

Metal spoon

Medium bowl

1 cup (240 ml) glass container with lid

1. If using juniper branches, cut off all the sprigs with scissors and discard any large branches. Then clean each sprig by lightly rinsing it with cool water for 1 to 2 minutes. Remove and discard any juniper berries and excess debris. Let the branches dry completely for at least 24 hours.

2. Line a sheet pan with aluminum foil and set it on the ground where you'll prepare the juniper ash outside. Place the campfire grill grate directly over the sheet pan, so that the entire sheet pan is underneath the grill grate without any obstructions. You should be able to easily remove the sheet pan from underneath the grill grate.

4. Once all the ashes have cooled for 8 to 10 minutes, carefully remove the sheet pan from underneath the grill grate and discard any debris left on the top of the grill.

3. Place 3 to 5 sprigs on top of the grill grate. Then, with a kitchen torch, fully ignite the juniper sprigs so that they burn completely. The juniper embers will fall onto the sheet pan underneath the grill grate. Repeat, working in batches of 3 to 5 sprigs, being careful to control the open flames. The branch portion of the juniper sprig will mostly remain on the grill while the burned cedar embers will fall onto the sheet pan.

5. Carefully scoop the ashes into the sifter with a metal spoon and sift the ash into the bowl.

6. Store the juniper ash in an airtight glass container in a cool place, such as a pantry, for up to 6 months.

How to Roast Green Chiles

Roasted green chiles are common to New Mexican cooking and southwestern cuisines. When I went off to college in the Midwest, I was perplexed how no one knew what I meant by green chiles. My friends often said, "Oh, you mean jalapeños?" My response was a little laugh followed by a "NO!" It never occurred to me how unique green chiles are to New Mexico, specifically Hatch green chiles. These chiles can range from mild to medium, to hot to extra hot, and roasting the chiles deepens the flavor even more. Depending on your liking for hot foods, you can pick your preferred heat level. However, one of the distinguishing features of Hatch green chiles is how hot they are! One of my favorite fall meals is Green Chile Stew (page 77).

Green chiles are typically harvested in fall, from early September to early October. During this time, the New Mexican air smells of deliciously fragrant roasted green chiles. It's one of my favorite fall scents, next to pumpkin spice. Usually, grocery stores and farms offer complimentary roasting for their green chiles, which are often purchased in large quantities. These roasted chiles are then cleaned, packaged, and stored frozen for use year-round.

In recent years, Hatch green chiles have gained popularity nationwide, and a lot of grocery stores will carry fresh Hatch green chiles during the fall. That is the best time to stock up. If you miss the harvest season, you can opt for frozen green chiles, which are typically found in the frozen foods section of your local grocery store. The next-best options are the bottled or canned varieties of Hatch green chiles that can usually be found near the bottled salsas or in the international/Mexican food aisles. However, please note bottled and canned varieties may also have added flavors to preserve them. Frozen and fresh varieties can be purchased online from Hatch green chile farmers as well.

If you cannot find Hatch green chiles, you can substitute Anaheim or poblano peppers, both of which can be found in the produce section of your grocery store. These peppers are similar to Hatch green chiles but are often way milder in spice level. I share quite a few recipes that require roasted green chiles like Green Chile Stew (page 77), Squash, Corn, and Green Chile Bowls (page 98), and the Lamb Sandwich (page 90).

This is an easy way to roast green chiles at home. Please note: if you are sensitive to capsaicin (the compound in chiles that makes them hot), or if you are roasting green chiles that are medium, hot, or extra hot, it is best to wear gloves while handling them.

1. Place a rack at the top of the oven. Preheat the oven to a high broil.

2. Line a sheet pan with aluminum foil.

3. Rinse and clean the green chiles called for in the recipe with cool water for 1 to 2 seconds. Scrub any debris away with your hands and place the chiles in a large colander with a kitchen towel underneath to absorb any excess water.

4. Dry each chile completely with a kitchen towel. Place the chiles in a single layer onto the prepared sheet pan, leaving about ½ inch (1 cm) between each chile.

5. Broil for 6 to 8 minutes, until the chile skins start to darken and blister. Remove from the oven and turn over the chiles with metal tongs. If the chiles are rather large and are too close to the heating element, adjust the oven rack to a lower level.

6. Place the chiles back into the oven and broil for another 6 to 8 minutes, until the chile skins start to darken and blister. Remove from the oven.

7. Add the freshly roasted green chiles to a large heat-safe bowl and cover with a heat-safe plate. Let the chiles sit for at least 10 minutes, or until the chile skins pull away easily.

8. With tongs or gloved hands, carefully remove the chiles and peel the skin off all the chiles. Discard the chile skins.

9. With a paring knife, cut off and discard the stems. Then cut the chile lengthwise to expose the seeds. Remove the seeds by lightly scraping with a knife or a spoon. Discard the seeds.

10. Use the chiles immediately. If you are planning to save the chiles for later, you can dice them up to your liking or freeze them in strips. Add the cleaned chiles to a freezer bag in a single layer. These can be kept frozen for up to 1 year.

How to Roast Cornmeal

Roasted cornmeal is the key to making delicious and flavorful corn dishes, and it is used for all the corn recipes that I share. Typically, roasted cornmeal is made by roasting the kernels prior to stone-grinding them into a meal. One common question I get on my blog is whether raw or unroasted cornmeal can be used instead. You can absolutely use it; however, it may be lacking in flavor and color. Roasting deepens not only the color of the cornmeal but also its flavor and the aromatics of the corn by adding a bit of a smoky and nutty flavor.

If you cannot find roasted (blue, white, and yellow) cornmeal, this is a quick and easy way to roast it at home. Since a majority of my recipes require less than 3 cups (540 g) of cornmeal for each recipe, I recommend roasting your cornmeal as you need it. However, you can store your roasted cornmeal in an airtight container in a cool, dark pantry for up to 1 month. I like to roast cornmeal in a pan on the stove as it's easier to handle and prevents overtoasting. As noted earlier in this section, please make sure the cornmeal is stone-ground.

1. Preheat a large pan or cast-iron skillet over medium heat for 3 to 5 minutes.

2. Add the amount of cornmeal needed for the recipe, plus an extra ¼ cup (45 g) to account for any spilled cornmeal. Don't exceed 3 cups (540 g) of cornmeal at a time.

3. With a wooden spoon, evenly spread the cornmeal around the pan. Let it toast for 4 to 5 minutes and stir, continuing until the cornmeal turns a shade darker. Remove the pan and adjust the heat if the cornmeal starts to burn.

4. Transfer the roasted cornmeal to a medium or large bowl and let it cool completely uncovered. You can use it once it feels cool to the touch.

Unroasted cornmeal

Roasted cornmeal

Cooking Outside

Traditionally, Navajo food was primarily cooked outside on an open fire. Depending on what was being made, food was roasted on the open fire directly, or it was cooked directly on top of the fire embers. Stone griddles were used to make flat corn bread. Navajo clay pots were used to boil foods. Sometimes small pits were dug and the food was baked beneath the fire embers, creating a little oven. Simple foods were made like corn breads and mushes. This type of cooking isn't as common today, but my mom would tell me stories about how my grandma would make biscuits in the fire embers when she was younger.

Cooking in large oven pits is also a traditional way of Navajo cooking that is still practiced today. These underground oven pits are often used for traditional Navajo ceremonies and cooking traditional Navajo foods, like to bake the 'alkaad at a kinaaldá. Deeper underground pits are used during the harvest season to cook large batches of corn for the steamed corn that is then used to make dried steamed corn and kneel down bread. These pits all require an open fire above the pit, and a lot of time and responsibility is needed to maintain the fire while cooking these foods.

Cooking over a grill is a more modern way of making Navajo food, but it still implements the method of using a fire. Each grill is unique to each family, but most families have some type of over-the-fire grill. To control the heat, rocks are often used to build a U-shaped border around the fire to hold in the heat and act as a base for the grill grate. Standing grills and more commercial types of grills are quite common as well. One of the distinguishing features of Navajo cooking is that wood is the preferred choice for cooking food. A lot of the time oak and juniper branches are used.

Almost any meal can be cooked outside. For example, people often choose to make fry bread outside to avoid the lingering smell of the oil. It is also best to cook larger pieces of meat outside like mutton and lamb ribs because there is more room on the grill.

There are many benefits to cooking outside. Not only does cooking food on an open fire help to deepen the flavors of the food, but it's also a fun way to spend time with your family. From the summer cookouts and fall harvests to traditional ceremonies, the act of being around an open fire reminds me of family and how it brings us together. As an adult, I realize the importance of cooking outside and how it connects you with nature. I feel like I am cooking a meal alongside my ancestors and I remember the teachings of my family. It's one of the ways I practice hózhǫ, or harmony and balance.

That is because everyone participates in the activity, even if they aren't cooking. Someone needs to gather and prepare the firewood. Meanwhile, others are in the kitchen preparing the items to be cooked. When the fire gets started, everyone is drawn to the fire. I was always taught to feed the fire as a way of giving thanks—a teaching that was passed on by my ancestors. Then we all gather and share stories and help along with the cooking or tending to the fire. I remember feeling so special whenever my mom or grandma gave me a piece of the first tortilla made on the grill. Fresh bread made outside will always be my favorite meal because of that.

Lupton, Arizona

Bááh Danilínígíí
BREADS

Navajo breads were the first thing I learned to make, and it was an easy way to help in the kitchen. Some of my favorite memories are around the stove or open fire making bread with my family. It is a communal activity that includes the eldest to the youngest, and I always enjoy the conversations I have when making bread. It is often my choice of therapy after a long day or a way to catch up with shimá when I visit the family home. As a mom, I carry on bread-making with my daughter. It makes me smile seeing her misshaped bread and it reminds me of the bread that I once made when I was her age.

Náneeskaadí
Navajo Tortillas

Tortillas, or náneeskaadí, are a staple bread in Navajo cooking. Navajo tortillas are usually thicker than Mexican tortillas. However, the thickness varies depending on where you are on the Navajo Nation. I grew up eating thin tortillas, and that's how I prepare mine. Traditional Navajo tortillas are not made with olive oil, but I find it makes the dough softer.

Yield: 8 servings	Prep time: 20 minutes	Cook time: 10 minutes

3 cups (360 g) all-purpose flour, plus more as needed

1½ teaspoons baking powder

½ teaspoon salt

½ teaspoon extra-virgin olive oil

1½ cups (360 ml) warm water

1. In a medium bowl, mix together the flour, baking powder, and salt with your hands until fully combined.

2. Add the olive oil and incorporate it into the dry mixture with your hands.

3. Slowly pour in 1 cup (240 ml) of the water and mix it in by hand. Then slowly add in another ¼ cup (60 ml) of the water and start to form the mixture into a ball. If there are still dry ingredients at the bottom of the bowl, add the remaining ¼ cup (60 ml) water and mix until all the ingredients are combined. If the dough is really sticking to your hands, add more flour, a tablespoon at a time, until it no longer sticks. You will know that the dough is the right consistency when it is tacky but can be easily pulled away from your hands while mixing. Knead the dough for 3 to 5 minutes, until it no longer sticks to the sides of the bowl. Cover the dough and let it rest for 10 minutes.

4. Preheat a large pan or cast-iron skillet over medium heat for 5 to 6 minutes. While the pan is heating up, divide the dough into eight balls. Place the dough balls back in the bowl and sprinkle them with a tablespoon of flour. Take one dough ball and, using either your hands or a rolling pin, stretch or roll the dough into a 7- to 8-inch (18 to 20 cm) round that is ⅛ to ¼ inch (3 to 6 mm) thick.

5. Carefully place the dough round on the pan and let it cook for about 1 minute, or until small bubbles form on the top. Flip and cook on the other side for 1 minute. Repeat with the remaining dough. Serve warm.

Dah Díníilghaazh
Fry Bread

Fry bread is one of the most popular Native American foods. In the Navajo language we call it dah díníilghaazh. It is a food that was created out of resilience and is a celebratory bread made at family celebrations and public events. Each tribe has their own version of fry bread. Navajo fry bread is usually large and thin and is traditionally deep-fried in shortening or lard, but my preference is to use canola oil, as I find it less greasy and healthier. It is the perfect base for a Lamb Sandwich (page 90) or to dip into Mutton and Vegetable Stew (page 69). For a sweeter option, you can drizzle it with Sumac Berry Jam (page 119) or Berry Compote (page 123).

For crisp fry bread, leave the fry bread uncovered. For soft fry bread, cover with a lid or a dish towel until ready to serve.

Yield: 8 servings	Prep time: 20 minutes	Cook time: 10 minutes

3 cups (360 g) all-purpose flour, plus more as needed

1½ teaspoons baking powder

½ teaspoon salt

1½ cups (360 ml) warm water

Canola oil, for frying

1. In a medium bowl, mix together the flour, baking powder, and salt with your hands until fully combined.

2. Slowly pour 1 cup (240 ml) of the water into the bowl and mix it in by hand. Then slowly add another ¼ cup (60 ml) of the water and start to form the mixture into a ball. If there are still dry ingredients at the bottom of the bowl, add the remaining ¼ cup (60 ml) water and mix until all the ingredients are combined. If the dough is sticking to your hands, add more flour, a tablespoon at a time, until the dough is no longer so sticky. You will know that the dough is the right consistency when it is tacky but can be easily pulled away from your hands while mixing.

3. Knead the dough for 3 to 5 minutes, until it no longer sticks to the sides of the bowl. Cover the dough and let rest for 10 minutes.

4. Divide the dough into eight equal balls. Place the dough balls back into the bowl and cover.

5. In a medium skillet or cast-iron pan, add enough oil until it reaches halfway up the pan or there are about 2 inches (5 cm) of oil. Heat the oil on medium-high heat until it reaches about 350°F (180°C). (Test the oil by taking a small piece of the dough and putting it in the oil; if the dough turns golden brown within a few seconds, the oil is ready to use.)

6. Take 1 dough ball and, using either your hands or a rolling pin, stretch or roll the dough into a 7- to 8-inch (18 to 20 cm) round that is ⅛ to ¼ inch (3 to 6 mm) thick. With a fork or your finger, poke a small hole in the center of the dough round and carefully place the dough in the hot oil.

7. Let the dough cook for 10 to 20 seconds on each side, until it turns golden brown. Transfer the fry bread to a paper towel–lined plate to remove excess oil. Repeat with the remaining dough balls. Serve warm.

Bááh Nímazí
Biscuits

Biscuits, or bááh nímazí, may also be referred to as "oven bread" on the Navajo Nation. In the olden days, though, since ovens weren't available, the dough was cooked in the embers of a hot fire. Unlike traditional American cut-out biscuits, these are formed into patties with your hands. These biscuits are wide and thin and are sometimes used to make sandwiches. I enjoy them with a crunchy crust, but if a softer crust is desired, brush olive oil or butter on the top before baking. Serve for breakfast or with a stew.

Yield: 8 servings	Prep time: 20 minutes	Cook time: 15 minutes

3 cups (360 g) all-purpose flour, plus more as needed

1½ teaspoons baking powder

½ teaspoon salt

½ teaspoon extra-virgin olive oil

1½ cups (360 ml) warm water

Sumac Berry Jam (page 119), for serving

1. Preheat the oven to 425°F (220°C). Line a sheet pan with parchment paper or aluminum foil.

2. In a medium bowl, mix together the flour, baking powder, salt, and olive oil with your hands until fully combined.

3. Slowly pour in 1 cup (240 ml) of the warm water to the dry mixture and mix it in by hand. Then slowly add another ¼ cup (60 ml) of water and start to form the mixture into a ball. If there are still dry ingredients at the bottom of the bowl, add the remaining ¼ cup (60 ml) water and mix until all the ingredients are combined. If the dough is really sticking to your hands, add more flour, a tablespoon at a time, until it no longer sticks. You will know that the dough is the right consistency when it is tacky but can be easily pulled away from your hands while mixing.

4. Knead the dough for 3 to 5 minutes, until it no longer sticks to the sides of the bowl. Cover the dough and let it rest for 10 minutes.

5. Form the biscuits by dividing the dough into eight balls. Flatten each ball into patties that are 3 inches (8 cm) in diameter and about ½ inch (1 cm) thick. Space them evenly on the prepared sheet pan.

6. Bake for 15 to 18 minutes, until the tops of the biscuits are golden brown. Let the biscuits cool for at least 5 minutes, until cool enough to handle.

7. Serve warm with sumac berry jam.

Bááh Dootłʼizhí
Blue Corn Patties

This recipe has only four ingredients, yet it packs a lot of flavor. Traditionally, these are made outside on a hot flat stone that acts like a griddle. Elders like to dip these blue corn patties into mutton stew. I enjoy having these as a snack with Navajo Tea (page 149).

Yield: 6 servings	Prep time: 15 minutes	Cook time: 10 minutes

2 teaspoons juniper ash (see page 23)

½ teaspoon salt

1½ cups (270 g) roasted blue cornmeal (see page 27)

1. In a medium saucepan, combine the juniper ash and ½ cup (120 ml) of water and mix with a wooden spoon. Bring the mixture to a boil over medium heat and let it boil for 3 to 4 minutes, until the mixture turns a gray color and is bubbling hot. Remove from the heat and add the salt. Mix well.

2. Stir in the cornmeal, ½ cup (90 g) at a time. Once all the cornmeal is incorporated, add ¼ cup (60 ml) cool water and continue to mix until a thick dough forms.

3. Transfer the dough to a medium heat-safe bowl and let it cool for 3 to 4 minutes, until it is cool enough to handle.

4. Heat a medium pan or cast-iron skillet over medium heat for 8 minutes.

5. While the pan is preheating, mix the dough with your hands for 2 minutes and then divide the dough into six balls. Flatten each ball into a round patty about 3 inches (8 cm) in diameter and ¼ inch (6 mm) thick. Place the patties on a plate and cover with a damp paper towel.

6. Cook the patties for 4 to 5 minutes on each side, until slightly toasted and deep blue in color. If the patties start to toast quickly, reduce the heat to medium-low. Serve warm with stew.

Bááh Dootł'izhí
Blue Corn Bread

This recipe is a modern version of Blue Corn Patties (page 38). It is similar to traditional yellow corn bread but uses blue cornmeal, which is less sweet than yellow cornmeal. The corn bread is light and fluffy and pairs well with Three Sisters Stew (page 78) and Chili Beans (page 74). It is also the base for Blue Corn Bread Stuffing (page 111). For this recipe, I intentionally left out the juniper ash.

Yield: 9 servings	Prep time: 10 minutes	Cook time: 22 minutes

1 cup (180 g) roasted blue cornmeal (see page 27)

1 cup (120 g) all-purpose flour

2 teaspoons baking powder

¼ cup (50 g) sugar

½ teaspoon salt

1 large egg

1 cup (240 ml) milk

¼ cup vegetable oil (60 ml) or melted unsalted butter

Piñons (optional)

1. Preheat the oven to 350°F (180°C). Coat the inside of an 8-inch (20 cm) square baking dish with nonstick spray.

2. In a medium bowl, whisk together the cornmeal, flour, baking powder, sugar, and salt until well combined.

3. In a small bowl, whisk together the egg, milk, and oil until well combined.

4. Pour the wet ingredients into the dry ingredients and whisk them together until the mixture is smooth.

5. Pour the batter into the prepared baking dish and bake for 20 to 22 minutes, until the bread is golden brown and a toothpick inserted in the center comes out clean.

6. Let cool for 5 minutes before serving. Top with piñons, if desired.

Nitsidigo'í
Kneel Down Bread

Kneel down bread, or nitsidigo'i, is a traditional Navajo white corn bread that is wrapped in a husk and cooked in a large firepit in the ground. Traditionally, Navajo women would sit in a kneeling position to grind the fresh corn on a grinding stone, which is where this bread gets its name. Today, most kneel down bread is made with a grain mill grinder as it is usually produced in large batches after the fall harvest.

This recipe calls for fresh Navajo white corn, which can be found during the fall at local flea markets and farmers' markets on the Navajo Nation. Please note that Navajo white corn, which is a type of dent corn, is different from the typical sweet corn found in grocery stores.

Yield: 8 servings	Prep time: 25 minutes	Cook time: 1 hour

6 ears fresh Navajo white corn with husks

1 teaspoon salt

2 teaspoons extra-virgin olive oil

1. Place a rack in the middle of the oven and preheat the oven to 350°F (180°C). Line a sheet pan with aluminum foil.

2. Husk the corn: First cut off the bottom part of the corn with a chef's knife, about 1 inch (2.5 cm) from the base. Then slice down the middle of the husks from the top to bottom. Carefully peel the husks off the corn. The husks will be used as baking vessels, so try to keep them in one large sheet. Discard the silk.

3. Clean each husk by rinsing it with cold water for 10 to 20 seconds to remove any dirt or debris. Place the cleaned husks in a large bowl and set aside.

4. With a knife, carefully cut all the kernels off the cobs and place them in a large bowl.

5. Pour the corn kernels, along with any liquid that has accumulated, into a food processor and pulse for 1 to 2 minutes, until a clumpy mush forms. It is important not to overpulse the mixture.

6. Transfer the corn mush to a large bowl, add the salt and olive oil, and mix with a wooden spoon until evenly combined. The mixture should resemble a thick mush and there should be very little liquid. If it looks soupy, remove some of the liquid with a spoon so that there is only about ¼ cup (60 ml) of corn milk. If the mixture has no liquid at all from the food-processed corn kernels, add ¼ cup (60 ml) of water at a time and mix until a thick mush is formed.

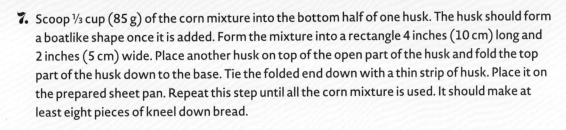

7. Scoop ⅓ cup (85 g) of the corn mixture into the bottom half of one husk. The husk should form a boatlike shape once it is added. Form the mixture into a rectangle 4 inches (10 cm) long and 2 inches (5 cm) wide. Place another husk on top of the open part of the husk and fold the top part of the husk down to the base. Tie the folded end down with a thin strip of husk. Place it on the prepared sheet pan. Repeat this step until all the corn mixture is used. It should make at least eight pieces of kneel down bread.

8. Bake for 30 minutes, then turn over and bake for another 30 minutes, until the bread is firm when touched.

9. Increase the oven temperature to 425°F (220°C) and bake for an additional 5 minutes, until the outer husks are toasted and lightly blackened.

10. Let the bread cool for at least 15 minutes. Serve warm with the corn husks removed.

Naadą́ą́' Dootł'izhí Náneeskaadí
Blue Corn Flour Tortillas

Blue corn flour tortillas are a fun, contemporary twist on traditional Navajo tortillas. The blue cornmeal adds more flavor, and the blue color brightens any dish. This recipe can make either eight mini tortillas or four large tortillas. I like making mini tacos with the mini tortillas. These tortillas pair well with Braised Red Chile Mutton Stew (page 80) or Lamb Meatballs (page 103).

Yield: 8 servings	Prep time: 20 minutes	Cook time: 16 minutes

1 cup (120 g) all-purpose flour

½ cup (90 g) roasted blue cornmeal (see page 27)

½ teaspoon baking powder

¼ teaspoon juniper ash (see page 23)

¼ teaspoon salt

1 tablespoon extra-virgin olive oil

1 cup (240 ml) warm water

1. In a medium bowl, mix together the flour, cornmeal, baking powder, juniper ash, and salt with your hands until combined.

2. Add the olive oil and incorporate it into the dry mixture with your hands.

3. Add ½ cup (120 ml) of the water and mix it in by hand. Then add another ¼ cup (60 ml) of the water and start to form the mixture into a ball. If the dough is still dry, add the remaining ¼ cup (60 ml) water.

4. Knead the dough for at least 4 minutes, or until the dough is smooth. Cover the dough and let it rest for 10 minutes.

5. While the dough is resting, heat a medium pan or cast-iron skillet over medium heat for 5 minutes.

6. Divide the dough into eight balls (or four balls for large tortillas). Then, with your hands or a rolling pin, stretch or roll the dough into rounds about 4 inches (10 cm) in diameter and ⅛ inch (3 mm) thick.

7. Place the dough round on the pan and cook for 1 minute on each side, until bubbles start to form and the tortilla looks lightly toasted. Repeat with the remaining dough. Serve warm.

Abínígo Daadánígíí
BREAKFAST

▶▶▶▶▶▶▶ ✦ ◀◀◀◀◀◀◀

I wanted to make sure to include this chapter, because when talking about Native American cuisine breakfast isn't commonly talked about, mostly because our meals are eaten any time of the day like Steam Corn Stew (page 73) and Potatoes and Ground Beef Bowls (page 97). However, when I was growing up, meals like blue corn mush, sumac berry pudding, and breakfast burritos were commonly eaten in the mornings. Since starting *The Fancy Navajo*, Navajo breakfast food fusions are one of my favorite recipes to share. These breakfast meals are quick and easy, and they offer lots of flavor.

Naadą́ą́' Dootł'izh Taa'niil
Blue Corn Mush Breakfast Fruit Bowl

Blue corn mush, or taa'niil, is a traditional Navajo food that combines blue cornmeal and juniper ash. Blue corn mush is served alone or with a sweetener or salt. I grew up eating it for breakfast, and my favorite way of enjoying it is by making a breakfast bowl and adding all my favorite toppings, such as strawberries, blueberries, chia seeds, pumpkin seeds, and honey. Depending on the season, I will change the fruit to whatever is most available. I personally like my mush thick, but if a thinner mush is desired, add an extra ½ cup (120 ml) water. If you want to try the savory version, then head to Savory Blue Corn Mush Bowl (page 83).

Yield: 4 servings	Prep time: 10 minutes	Cook time: 15 minutes

1 cup (180 g) roasted blue cornmeal (see page 27) 1 teaspoon juniper ash (see page 23) ½ cup (85 g) diced (about ¼ inch, or 6 mm) strawberries, for serving ½ cup (75 g) blueberries, for serving ¼ cup (40 g) chia seeds, for serving ½ cup (65 g) pumpkin seeds, for serving 4 teaspoons honey, for serving	**1.** In a medium bowl, whisk together the cornmeal and 1 cup (240 ml) of water until combined and set aside. **2.** In a medium saucepan, whisk together 2 cups (480 ml) of water and the juniper ash until combined. Bring the mixture to a boil over medium heat and let it boil for 5 minutes. Reduce the heat to medium-low. **3.** Slowly add the blue corn mixture to the juniper ash mixture, whisking continuously until fully combined. Be careful as the mush will immediately start to thicken and will splatter. Continue to cook for 3 to 5 minutes, until thickened. **4.** Ladle two scoops of the mush into each bowl and evenly distribute the toppings. Serve while hot.

Chiiłchin Naadą́ą́' Ak'áán bee Naashgizhkání
Sumac Berry Pudding

Chiiłchin is a sumac berry pudding that is commonly made with flour and ground sumac berries. It is usually served for breakfast but can be enjoyed any time of the day. Shimá did not make this at home very often. It was more of a treat to have at the Shiprock, New Mexico, flea market on a cold Saturday morning. Depending on how it's made, the consistency can be thick like a mush or thin like a beverage. Ground sumac berries have a slight lemony, tart flavor. This recipe incorporates white cornmeal, which provides a more roasted corn flavor. It is a very light and refreshing breakfast.

Yield: 4 servings	Prep time: 3 minutes	Cook time: 10 minutes

2 tablespoons ground sumac berries

¼ cup (45 g) white cornmeal

¼ cup (35 g) toasted pine nuts, for serving

Honey, sugar, and/or sweetener of your choice, for serving

1. In a medium saucepan, whisk together the ground sumac berries and 2 cups (480 ml) of water until combined. Bring the mixture to a boil over medium heat and let boil for 5 minutes.

2. Whisk the cornmeal, 1 tablespoon at a time, into the sumac mixture. Lower the heat to medium-low and cook for 5 to 8 minutes, stirring occasionally, until the mixture starts to thicken. Be careful as the mixture will start to splatter as it thickens.

3. Ladle the pudding into bowls. Sprinkle with pine nuts and serve with honey.

Naadą́ą́' Dootł'izhí Quiche
Blue Corn Quiche

This blue corn quiche is one of my go-to breakfasts when I want to feel extra fancy. I also like making this for Mother's Day or as a fun weekend treat.

Yield: 8 servings	Prep time: 30 minutes	Cook time: 50 minutes

2 teaspoons extra-virgin olive oil

¼ cup (35 g) diced (about ¼ inch, or 6 mm) yellow onion

½ cup (75 g) fresh yellow corn

1 cup (30 g) fresh spinach

5 large eggs

¼ cup (60 ml) milk

¼ teaspoon salt

½ cup (90 g) roasted blue cornmeal (see page 27)

¾ cup (90 g) all-purpose flour

⅓ cup (75 g) unsalted butter, thinly sliced

4 to 5 tablespoons ice water

½ cup (55 g) grated sharp cheddar cheese

1 large tomato, thinly sliced

¼ cup (25 g) grated Parmesan cheese

1. Place a rack in the middle of the oven and preheat the oven to 425°F (220°C).

2. Prepare the filling: In a large pan over medium heat, heat the olive oil for 2 to 3 minutes. Add the onion and cook for 3 to 4 minutes, until it starts to turn translucent. Add the corn and cook for 3 minutes. Add the spinach and cook for 2 minutes. Remove the pan from the heat and set aside.

3. In a medium bowl, whisk together the eggs, milk, and salt for 2 minutes, until combined. Set aside.

4. Prepare the crust: In a medium bowl, mix together the cornmeal and flour with your hands until combined. Using your hands, incorporate the butter into the cornmeal mixture until the butter turns into pea-size crumbles. Add 4 tablespoons of the cold water and start to form the mixture into a ball. If the dough feels a little dry, add the remaining tablespoon water. Try not to overwork the dough.

5. Flour a clean surface and rolling pin. Roll out the dough into a circle that is 10 to 11 inches (25 to 28 cm) in diameter. Transfer the dough to a 9-inch (23 cm) pie pan and cut off any excess dough with a knife.

6. Assemble the quiche: Place the cooked vegetable filling into the quiche shell. Sprinkle the cheddar on top. Pour in the egg mixture. Layer the top of the quiche with the sliced tomatoes. Sprinkle with the Parmesan.

7. Bake for 15 minutes to fully cook the crust, then lower the temperature to 350°F (180°C) and bake for an additional 25 minutes, until the eggs have set and the top is lightly toasted. Serve warm.

Atsị' SPAM/Yadiizíní Atsị' Náneeskadí Bił Yisdisí
SPAM/Canned Meat Breakfast Burrito

SPAM breakfast burritos are staples of modern Navajo cuisine. Some of my favorite memories are of waking up early to get a breakfast burrito from the burrito ladies along the roadside in Shiprock. They serve a variety of breakfast burritos that include meats like SPAM, bacon, sausage, corned beef, and ground beef, all from their parked vehicles. The burritos are usually wrapped in aluminum foil and served with a fresh jalapeño or serrano pepper.

Yield: 4 servings	Prep time: 10 minutes	Cook time: 20 minutes

2 tablespoons extra-virgin olive oil

3 medium russet potatoes, peeled and sliced into ¼-inch (6 mm) pieces

¼ teaspoon salt

¼ teaspoon ground black pepper

1 cup (225 g) diced (about ¼ inch, or 6 mm) SPAM

4 Navajo Tortillas (page 33)

4 large eggs, scrambled

1. In a large pan over medium heat, heat the olive oil for 2 minutes. Add the potatoes, salt, and pepper, mix together with a wooden spoon, then cook covered for 10 minutes, stirring occasionally.

2. Add the SPAM and cook covered for an additional 8 to 10 minutes, stirring occasionally, until the potatoes have softened and cooked through.

3. Assemble the burritos: To one tortilla, add ½ cup (113 g) of the SPAM and potato mixture. Then add ¼ cup (55 g) of the scrambled eggs. Fold in the sides over the filling and tuck in the bottom edges. Wrap the burritos in aluminum foil until ready to serve.

Alóós Cranberry bee Naashgizhkání

Rice Pudding with Cranberries

When I was growing up, this was one of shimá's favorite things to make in the morning. She made hers with milk and raisins, but I was never a fan of raisins. As an adult, I enjoy eating this with dried cranberries and oat milk instead. It's the perfect sweet breakfast option.

Yield: 4 to 6 servings	Prep time: 5 minutes	Cook time: 35 minutes

1 cup (185 g) white rice

3½ cups (840 ml) oat milk, plus more for serving if desired

½ cup (70 g) dried cranberries

Honey, sugar, and/or sweetener of your choice, for serving

1. In a medium mesh strainer, rinse the rice with cold water for 2 to 3 minutes, until the water starts to run clear.

2. Transfer the rice to a medium saucepan, add the oat milk, and bring the mixture to a boil over medium heat. Reduce the heat to medium-low and add the dried cranberries. Continue to cook for 15 to 20 minutes, stirring occasionally, until most of the oat milk has been absorbed.

3. Turn off the heat and cover the saucepan with a lid. Let the rice sit for 5 minutes.

4. Serve warm with honey and more oat milk (if desired).

Naadą́ą́' Ak'áán Granola
Corn Granola

Corn granola is a *fancy* Navajo version of traditional granola. It combines rolled oats, roasted blue cornmeal, and maple syrup. Granola is a weekly staple, and I love the addition of blue cornmeal. Alternatively, white or yellow roasted cornmeal can be used instead. The corn granola can be eaten on its own or used as a topping for yogurt parfaits. You can also add sliced almonds or pecans for extra crunch. For this recipe, it is best to use rolled oats; if you use the instant variety, you will not get the same result.

Yield: 3 cups (405 g)	Prep time: 5 minutes	Cook time: 22 minutes

¼ cup (60 ml) vegetable oil

½ cup (120 ml) maple syrup

1 tablespoon ground cinnamon

¼ teaspoon salt

3 cups (270 g) rolled oats

¾ cup (135 g) roasted blue cornmeal (see page 27)

1. Place a rack in the middle of the oven and preheat the oven to 325°F (170°C). Line a sheet pan with parchment paper.

2. In a medium bowl, mix together the oil, maple syrup, cinnamon, and salt with a rubber spatula or wooden spoon.

3. Add the oats and mix until they are evenly coated with the oil and maple syrup. Add the cornmeal and mix until evenly coated.

4. Pour the granola mixture onto the prepared sheet pan and spread it out evenly.

5. Bake the granola for 10 minutes. Take the sheet out of the oven and gently stir and flip over the granola. Bake for another 10 to 12 minutes, until the granola is nice and golden.

6. Let it cool for 10 to 15 minutes. The granola can be stored in a medium airtight container in a cool, dark pantry for up to 1 week.

'Abe' Bee Neezmasí
Blue Corn Pancakes

Blue corn pancakes are a staple not only of modern Navajo cuisine but also of southwestern cuisine. Traditional Navajo pancakes are typically thick and dense, but this modern version makes the fluffiest blue corn pancakes. The secret is the inclusion of Greek yogurt, which also adds protein. I like topping these with warm Berry Compote (page 123).

Yield: 8 pancakes	Prep time: 10 minutes	Cook time: 20 minutes

¾ cup (90 g) all-purpose flour

½ cup (90 g) roasted blue cornmeal (see page 27)

1 teaspoon baking powder

¼ teaspoon baking soda

¼ teaspoon salt

2 large eggs

1 cup (230 g) nonfat vanilla Greek yogurt

½ cup (120 ml) oat milk

2 tablespoons unsalted butter, melted

1 cup (230 g) Berry Compote (page 123), for serving

1. In a medium bowl, whisk together the flour, cornmeal, baking powder, baking soda, and salt until combined.

2. In a small bowl, whisk together the eggs, yogurt, oat milk, and melted butter until combined.

3. Add the wet ingredients to the dry ingredients and whisk until combined.

4. Warm up a medium pan or griddle over medium heat for 5 minutes.

5. Spray nonstick spray or add butter to the skillet. Scoop ¼ cup (60 ml) of the pancake batter onto the skillet and let it cook for 2 to 3 minutes, until bubbles start to form on the surface. Flip with a spatula and cook the other side for 1 to 2 minutes, until the bottom is a light brown color. Repeat with the remaining batter.

6. Serve warm with berry compote on top.

Naadą́ą́' Dootł'izhí Naayízí Waffle
Blue Corn Pumpkin Waffles

Waffles are not traditional to Navajo cuisine, but they are one of my favorite things to have on the weekend. These blue corn pumpkin waffles smell amazing, and they always make my house smell so good too! I like to make these during the fall. I top mine with maple syrup and nuts.

Yield: 4 to 5 waffles	Prep time: 10 minutes	Cook time: 20 minutes

½ cup (60 g) all-purpose flour

1 cup (180 g) roasted blue cornmeal (see page 27)

2 teaspoons baking powder

½ teaspoon juniper ash (see page 23)

¼ teaspoon salt

1 tablespoon sugar

1 large egg

¾ cup (180 ml) milk

4 tablespoons unsalted butter, melted

4 tablespoons pumpkin puree

1 teaspoon pumpkin pie spice

Maple syrup, for serving

Pumpkin seeds, pecans, almonds, pine nuts, or any other nuts of your choice, for serving

1. Preheat a waffle maker to medium-high heat.

2. In a large bowl, whisk together the flour, cornmeal, baking powder, juniper ash, and salt until combined.

3. In a medium bowl, whisk together the sugar, egg, milk, melted butter, pumpkin puree, and pumpkin pie spice until combined.

4. Add the wet ingredients to the dry ingredients and whisk until combined.

5. Spray the waffle maker with nonstick spray and scoop ⅓ to ½ cup (80 to 120 ml) of the batter into the waffle maker. Cook for 4 to 6 minutes, until steam no longer comes out of the waffle maker, or according to the manufacturer's instructions. Carefully remove the waffle and repeat with the remaining batter.

6. Serve with maple syrup and pumpkin seeds on top.

Naadą́'élgai Áłtsé Nit'į́į́h Bááhkání
White Corn Scones with Apricots

Apricots, or diłʼoodi, are a common Navajo fruit and are eaten fresh or dried. Together with the white cornmeal, these scones make for a delicious on-the-go meal.

Yield: 8 scones	Prep time: 15 minutes	Cook time: 22 minutes

SCONES

½ cup (120 ml) plus 2 tablespoons heavy cream

1 large egg

1 teaspoon vanilla extract

1 cup (120 g) all-purpose flour

1½ cups (270 g) roasted white cornmeal (see page 27)

1½ teaspoons baking powder

⅓ cup (65 g) granulated sugar

½ teaspoon salt

½ cup (150 g) cold unsalted butter, sliced

4 tablespoons apricot jam

¼ cup (50 g) organic cane sugar

GLAZE (optional)

½ cup (120 ml) heavy cream

2 tablespoons powdered sugar

1 tablespoon apricot jam

1. To make the scones: Place a rack in the middle of the oven and preheat the oven to 375°F (190°C). Line a sheet pan with parchment paper.

2. In a small bowl, whisk together ½ cup (120 ml) of the cream, the egg, and vanilla until combined. Set aside.

3. In a large bowl, whisk together the flour, cornmeal, baking powder, granulated sugar, and salt until combined. Add the butter to the flour mixture and mix with your hands until the butter is in pea-size pieces.

4. Slowly pour the cream mixture into the dry mixture and mix with your hands or a wooden spoon until a large dough ball is formed. Divide the dough in half and roll into balls.

5. Flour a clean surface and rolling pin. Roll out both dough balls into two disks that are 6 inches (15 cm) in diameter and ½ inch (1 cm) thick.

6. Add jam to the center of one of the dough disks. Evenly spread the jam, leaving about a ¼-inch (6 mm) border around the edges. Place the other dough disk on top so that the jam is now sandwiched between both disks. Lightly seal the two disks with your fingers. Cut the disk into eight triangles and place them on the prepared sheet pan.

7. Lightly brush the scones with the remaining 2 tablespoons cream and sprinkle the organic cane sugar on the tops.

8. Bake for 20 to 22 minutes, until the edges of the scones start to brown. Let the scones cool on the pan for 10 minutes.

9. If making the glaze: In a small bowl, whisk the cream and powdered sugar until combined. Add the apricot jam and whisk until combined. Drizzle onto the scones. Enjoy the scones warm.

Atoo' Ádaat'éhígíí
SOUPS & STEWS

Soups and stews bring the family together. Navajo soups and stews are made year-round and they are staples in Navajo cuisine. You commonly find a variety of stews at large celebrations like birthday parties, graduations, weddings, and traditional ceremonies. Whenever my family and I visit my childhood home, shimá always has stew and bread waiting for our arrival. It's the perfect "welcome home" meal. These are typically made in large batches, but these recipes are meant to be eaten in your weekday meals. I like to make these soups in a slow cooker in the morning and by the evening they are ready to eat.

Dibé Bitsį' 'Atoo'
Mutton and Vegetable Stew

Mutton stew or soup is a staple in Navajo cuisine. Typically, it is reserved for large gatherings and celebrations since a whole mutton backbone is used to make the stew. It is usually slow cooked for hours, and the backbone creates a lovely and savory broth. The smell of the stew is comforting and reminds me of home. You can also find mutton stew served at local flea markets on the weekends. It is typically served with Fry Bread (page 34) or Navajo Tortillas (page 33). If you cannot find mutton backbone, then cubed mutton stew meat can be used instead.

Yield: 8 to 10 servings	Prep time: 15 minutes	Cook time: 4 to 8 hours

2½ pounds (1.1 kg) mutton backbone, or 2 pounds (910 g) cubed mutton stew meat

3 large carrots, peeled and cut into ¼-inch (6 mm) slices

3 medium russet potatoes, peeled and cut into 1-inch (2.5 cm) cubes

4 medium celery stalks, cut into ¼-inch (6 mm) pieces

1 large white onion, diced into ¼-inch (6 mm) pieces

1½ teaspoons garlic powder

½ teaspoon salt

½ teaspoon ground black pepper

Fry Bread (page 34) or Navajo Tortillas (page 33), for serving

1. If using mutton backbone, rinse it with cold water. Slice along the bone line to make fillets.

2. In a 7- to 10-quart (6 to 9 L) slow cooker, place the mutton, carrots, potatoes, celery, onion, garlic powder, salt, and pepper.

3. Add 8 to 10 cups (1.9 to 2.4 L) of water, so that the water completely covers the mutton and vegetables. The water should be 2 to 3 inches (5 to 8 cm) above the vegetables and meat.

4. Cook on high for 4 to 6 hours or on low for 6 to 8 hours, until the meat is tender.

5. Ladle into soup bowls and enjoy hot with fry bread or tortillas.

K'íneeshbízhii 'Atoo'
Dumpling Stew

Dumpling stew, or k'íneeshbízhii, is what I like to call Navajo noodle soup. Traditionally, dumpling stew was made with cornmeal, but this version is more of a modern adaptation. My favorite part of this recipe is making the dumplings/noodles. It may sound complicated, but it's actually quite simple. This stew is served year-round, but I typically have it in the winter.

Yield: 4 to 6 servings	Prep time: 15 minutes	Cook time: 2½ hours

STEW

2 teaspoons extra-virgin olive oil

½ cup (65 g) diced (¼ inch, or 6 mm) yellow onion

1 pound (455 g) boneless cubed lamb stew meat or 1½ pounds (680 g) bone-in lamb stew meat

4 cups (960 ml) water or vegetable broth

1 teaspoon garlic powder

½ teaspoon salt

DUMPLINGS

1 cup (120 g) all-purpose flour

½ teaspoon salt

½ cup (120 ml) warm water

1. Prepare the stew: In a large pot over medium heat, warm up the olive oil for 5 minutes. Add the onion and cook for 3 to 4 minutes, until it starts to turn translucent.

2. Add the lamb and cook for 2 to 3 minutes, until browned and slightly seared.

3. Add the water, garlic powder, and salt and mix until combined. Bring the soup to a boil, then reduce the heat to medium-low, cover, and simmer for 2 hours.

4. After 2 hours, prepare the dumplings; you will want the dumplings to be as freshly made as possible. In a medium bowl, mix together the flour and salt with your hands until combined. Add the warm water to make a dough. Knead the dough for 2 minutes, until it no longer sticks to your hands.

5. Flour a clean surface and rolling pin. Roll the dough into a rectangle about 12 inches (30 cm) long, 6 inches (15 cm) wide, and ⅛ inch (3 mm) thick. With a knife, slice the dough vertically into ½-inch (1 cm) slices. It should resemble long flat noodles. Trim the dumplings horizontally, to about 2 inches (5 cm) long. They should be 2 inches (5 cm) long and ½ inch (1 cm) wide.

6. Add the dumplings to the soup and continue to cook for 15 to 20 minutes, until cooked through and no longer doughy. They should be firm and start to float to the top of the broth.

7. Ladle into soup bowls and serve immediately.

Neeshjízhii' 'Atoo'
Steam Corn Stew

Steam corn stew is a celebratory Navajo dish that is served for special occasions like birthdays or holidays. Neeshjízhii' is freshly harvested Navajo white corn that has been steamed in a firepit and then dried. Steam corn has an earthy, roasted corn flavor. Traditionally, the soup is made with mutton backbone and dried steam corn with no seasoning other than salt. This recipe is made with lamb stew meat, but beef stew meat can also be substituted. Steam corn is typically made during the fall season and can be purchased at local flea markets and trading posts on the Navajo Nation. Navajo farmers also sell it online. This soup is usually served with Fry Bread (page 34).

Yield: 8 to 10 servings	Prep time: 15 minutes	Cook time: 5 to 8 hours

1 cup dried steam corn

1 to 1½ pounds (455 to 680 g) lamb stew meat, cut into ½- to 1-inch (1 to 2.5 cm) cubes (1 pound if using boneless lamb stew meat, 1½ pounds if using bone-in)

½ teaspoon salt

½ teaspoon garlic powder

Fry Bread (page 34), for serving

1. Place the dried steam corn in a medium bowl and add cold water to cover. With your hands, clean and remove any debris from the steam corn in the water for 1 to 2 minutes. Drain and repeat this process two more times until the water is clear.

2. In a 7- to 10-quart (6 to 9 L) slow cooker, combine the lamb, drained steam corn, salt, and garlic powder. Add 8 to 10 cups (1.9 to 2.4 L) of water—the water should be 2 to 3 inches (5 to 8 cm) above the corn and meat. Cook for 5 to 6 hours on high or 7 to 8 hours on low, until the meat is tender and the corn is softened.

3. Ladle into bowls and serve hot with fry bread.

Naa'ołí Azeedích'íí'

Chili Beans

Growing up we didn't eat a lot of beans, but when we did it was always when shimá made chili beans for Navajo Tacos (page 93). She would slow cook them all day and the house would smell amazing! This recipe uses dried pinto beans, a Navajo pantry staple, together with ground beef and red chile. It's the perfect recipe for chili beans and can be eaten alone as a soup or used as a topping for Navajo Tacos (page 93).

Yield: 8 to 10 servings	Prep time: 15 minutes, plus overnight soaking of beans	Cook time: 6 to 8 hours

2 cups (390 g) dried pinto beans

4 cups (960 ml) vegetable broth or water

1 teaspoon salt

2 tablespoons New Mexico red chile powder

1 tablespoon garlic powder

1 tablespoon onion powder

1 teaspoon ground cumin

1 pound (455 g) ground beef

¼ cup (65 g) tomato paste

1 can (14.5 ounces, or 411 g) diced tomatoes

1. Prepare the beans by rinsing them in cold water for 2 minutes to remove any debris. Add the beans to a medium bowl and cover completely with water so that there are 3 to 4 inches (8 to 10 cm) of water above the beans. Cover and let sit on the counter overnight.

2. The next day, drain and rinse the beans with cold water.

3. In a 7- to 10-quart (6 to 9 L) slow cooker, stir together the beans, vegetable broth, salt, chile powder, garlic powder, onion powder, and cumin. Cook on high for 4 to 5 hours or on low for 6 to 8 hours, until the beans are tender.

4. Thirty minutes before the beans are done, prepare the meat. In a large skillet over medium heat, cook the beef for 8 to 10 minutes, until browned. Drain any grease and add the beef to the slow cooker along with the tomato paste and canned tomatoes. Stir and slow cook for an additional 30 minutes on high, until the broth starts to thicken.

5. Ladle into soup bowls or use to make Navajo tacos.

Atoo' Azeedích'ííłtł'izhí bił
Green Chile Stew

Green chile stew is not a traditional Navajo recipe. But I grew up in New Mexico, and a lot of Navajo cuisine includes New Mexico Hatch green chiles. Almost every Navajo meal includes some sort of chile. I personally love a spicy stew and this one is best made in the fall, when it is green chile roasting season.

This recipe calls for Hatch green chiles, which are common to New Mexico. When they're not in season, you can find frozen Hatch green chiles at grocery stores. This stew can be served with Navajo Tortillas (page 33).

Yield: 8 to 10 servings	Prep time: 15 minutes	Cook time: 45 minutes

1 pound (455 g) ground beef	**1.** In a large pot over medium-high heat, cook the ground beef for 6 to 10 minutes, until browned. Drain the grease so that only 2 teaspoons of fat are left in the pot.
1 medium white onion, diced into ¼-inch (6 mm) pieces	
4 cloves garlic, minced	**2.** Return the pot to the stove, add the onions, garlic, salt, and pepper, and cook over medium-high heat for 5 to 8 minutes, until the onions are softened.
½ teaspoon salt	
½ teaspoon ground black pepper	
3 medium russet potatoes, peeled and cut into 1-inch (2.5 cm) cubes	**3.** Add the potatoes, tomatoes and their liquid, green chiles, and beef broth. Mix together and bring to a boil. Lower the heat to medium and cook for 30 to 35 minutes, until the potatoes are cooked through.
1 can (14.5 ounces, or 411 g) diced tomatoes	
1 cup (150 g) chopped roasted mild or hot Hatch green chiles (see page 25)	**4.** Ladle into bowls and serve with tortillas.
4 cups (960 ml) beef broth	
Navajo Tortillas (page 33), for serving	

Táá' Ałdeezhí Atoo'
Three Sisters Stew

"Three sisters" refers to the traditional gardening method used by Indigenous tribes, in which corn, beans, and squash are grown together. The best time to have a three sisters feast is during harvest season in the fall. There is nothing like freshly harvested corn and squash with beans that have been slow cooking all day. This particular stew came into fruition because I craved these same flavors during the spring and summer months when Navajo squash and white corn are no longer in season. Serve with Fry Bread (page 34) or Blue Corn Bread (page 41).

Yield: 8 to 10 servings	Prep time: 15 minutes	Cook time: 40 minutes

2 tablespoons extra-virgin olive oil

1 cup (118 g) diced (about ¼ inch, or 6 mm) yellow onion

1 tablespoon minced garlic

1 teaspoon salt

1 cup (115 g) diced (about ¼ inch, or 6 mm) zucchini

2½ cups (288 g) diced (about ¼ inch, or 6 mm) yellow squash

1 teaspoon dried thyme

½ teaspoon ground black pepper

1 can (15 ounces, or 425 g) white corn, drained and rinsed

1 can (15.5 ounces, or 439 g) pinto beans, drained and rinsed

4 cups (960 ml) vegetable broth

¼ cup (45 g) white cornmeal

Fry Bread (page 34) or Blue Corn Bread (page 41), for serving

1. In a large pot over medium heat, heat the olive oil for 1 minute. Add the onions, garlic, and salt. Cook and stir for about 5 minutes, or until the onions are translucent.

2. Add the zucchini, yellow squash, thyme, and pepper and cook and stir for 5 minutes, or until the squash has softened.

3. Add the white corn, pinto beans, and vegetable broth and bring to a boil over medium heat. Let boil for 10 minutes, stirring occasionally.

4. Meanwhile, in a small bowl, whisk together the cornmeal and ¼ cup (60 ml) of water until combined.

5. Add half of the cornmeal mixture to the soup and mix until combined, then add the remaining cornmeal mixture and mix until combined. Return the soup to a boil, then reduce the heat to medium-low and cook for 20 minutes, or until the soup thickens and the vegetables are cooked through.

6. Ladle into soup bowls and serve with fry bread or blue corn bread.

Azeedích'íílchí'í Dibé Bitsį' Ak'ah Bii' Yizaazgo dóó Tó Áłchx'įįdígo Bee Shibéezhí

Braised Red Chile Mutton Stew

This is the perfect stew to make on weekends. Braised red chile mutton stew is a contemporary take on mutton stew. It infuses the flavors of the New Mexico red chile and Navajo white cornmeal into a soft and tender stew. I like serving it with freshly made Blue Corn Flour Tortillas (page 45) or alongside a Savory Blue Corn Mush Bowl (page 83).

Yield: 4 servings	Prep time: 30 minutes	Cook time: 3 hours

8 dried mild or hot New Mexico red chiles

3 cups (720 ml) hot water

6 garlic cloves, peeled

2 pounds (910 g) mutton or lamb loin chops

2 teaspoons extra-virgin olive oil

1 teaspoon salt

2 tablespoons brown sugar

2 tablespoons white cornmeal

Blue Corn Flour Tortillas (page 45) or Savory Blue Corn Mush Bowl (page 83), for serving

1. Place a rack in the middle of the oven and preheat the oven to 300°F (150°C).

2. Prepare the dried chiles by giving them a quick rinse under warm water for about 1 minute each. Remove and discard the stems and seeds.

3. Place the rinsed chiles and hot water in a blender. Let the mixture sit for 5 minutes. Then add the garlic and blend on medium speed for 3 to 4 minutes, until fully blended. Strain the mixture through a fine-mesh strainer into a medium bowl and set it aside. Discard any seeds and sediment in the strainer.

4. Prepare the lamb by trimming any excess fat with a knife. I like to leave on 10 to 15 percent of the fat.

5. Warm up a large pan or cast-iron skillet over medium-high heat for 4 to 5 minutes. Add the olive oil. Add the lamb chops and sear on each side for 2 minutes. Place the lamb chops into a 9-inch (23 cm) square baking dish and set aside.

6. Pour the reserved red chile sauce into the pan used to sear the meat and bring it to a boil over medium heat. Whisk in the salt and brown sugar and continue to boil the sauce for 5 minutes. Reduce the heat to low.

7. Slowly whisk the cornmeal into the sauce, a tablespoon at a time. Cook, stirring continuously, for 5 minutes, until the sauce is thickened.

8. Pour the red chile sauce over the lamb chops and place in the oven for 3 hours, until the meat is soft and easily pulls away from the bone. The internal temperature of the meat should be 170°F (77°C).

9. Serve warm with blue corn tortillas or a savory blue corn mush bowl.

Naadą́ą́' Dootł'izh Taa'niil
Savory Blue Corn Mush Bowl

This blue and white corn mush bowl is a revitalized twist on blue corn mush. When I was growing up, corn mush was mostly eaten as a breakfast food. It was very rare to have white or yellow corn mush, as blue was the most popular. Traditionally, though, cornmeal mush was eaten at any time of the day. This recipe combines blue and yellow corn mush with butter and green chiles to make a delicious and savory meal.

Yield: 4 servings	Prep time: 20 minutes	Cook time: 30 minutes

½ cup (90 g) roasted blue cornmeal (see page 27)	**1.** In a medium bowl, whisk together the blue cornmeal and ½ cup (120 ml) of water until combined. Set aside.
½ cup (90 g) roasted white cornmeal (see page 27)	**2.** In another medium bowl, whisk together the white cornmeal and ½ cup (120 ml) of water until combined. Set aside.
1 teaspoon juniper ash (see page 23)	**3.** In a medium saucepan, whisk together 1¼ cups (300 ml) of water and ½ teaspoon of the juniper ash until combined. Bring the mixture to a boil over medium heat and let it boil for 5 minutes, until the juniper ash has fully dissolved and the mixture has come to a roaring boil. Reduce the heat to medium-low.
Salted butter, for serving	
Chopped roasted Hatch green chiles (see page 25), for serving	**4.** Slowly add the blue corn mixture to the saucepan, whisking continuously until fully combined. Be careful as the mush will immediately start to thicken and may splatter.
	5. Using a separate saucepan, repeat steps 3 and 4 with the white cornmeal.
	6. Continue to cook both the blue and white corn mush separately for 3 to 5 minutes, until thickened.
	7. Ladle one scoop of the blue corn mush and one scoop of the white corn mush into each bowl.
	8. Top with salted butter and green chile to your liking.

Nímasii dóó Atsį' Spam Atoo'
Potato and SPAM Soup

Shimá would prepare this soup on busy weekdays when she wanted a quick and easy meal. She would make a simple flour gravy, but shínaaí (my brother), who shared this version of the recipe, makes a fancy buttered roux that adds more flavor to the dish.

Yield: 4 servings	Prep time: 10 minutes	Cook time: 35 minutes

4 medium russet potatoes

2 tablespoons extra-virgin olive oil

½ cup (65 g) diced yellow onion

1 teaspoon salt

½ teaspoon black pepper

2 cups (450 g) diced (about ¼ inch, or 6 mm) SPAM

2 tablespoons unsalted butter

4 tablespoons all-purpose flour

½ cup (30 g) chopped green onions, for serving

Navajo Tortillas (page 33), for serving

1. Peel and rinse the potatoes, then cut them into ¼-inch (6 mm) quarter-moon slices.

2. Transfer the potatoes to a colander and rinse with cold water.

3. In a medium bowl, combine the potatoes and ¼ cup (60 ml) of water. Set aside.

4. In a large pot over medium-high heat, warm up the olive oil for 5 minutes. Add the onion, salt, and pepper and cook for 2 to 3 minutes, until the onions are softened.

5. Add the potato and water mixture to the pot, cover, and cook for 10 minutes, stirring frequently.

6. Add the SPAM to the pot and let it cook for 5 minutes.

7. Transfer the SPAM and potato mixture to a medium heat-safe bowl. Set aside.

8. Meanwhile, make the roux. Reduce the heat to medium-low. Add the butter to the pot. Once it melts, add the flour, 1 tablespoon at a time, while stirring continuously with a wooden spoon. Let the flour mixture cook for 3 to 5 minutes, until it turns a light brown color. Add 2½ cups (600 ml) of water and stir until smooth.

9. Add the SPAM and potato mixture back to the pot. Increase the heat to medium and cook for another 5 minutes, until the soup is lightly thickened.

10. Ladle into soup bowls and sprinkle with the green onions. Enjoy with tortillas.

Íyisí Daadánígíí
MAIN DISHES

This section is a combination of dishes that tie modern and traditional Navajo cuisine together. A lot of the main dishes I ate while I was growing up were simple, yet full of flavor. They were easy dishes that shimá made during the week or that we picked up at the local flea market. The recipes featured in this chapter not only incorporate traditional Navajo flavors, but are also fused with modern ingredients.

Dibé Bitsį'
Traditional Mutton Ribs

Mutton ribs are a traditional delicacy reserved for large family gatherings and celebrations. Some of my favorite memories growing up were when shimásaní would butcher a whole sheep for the family. It was an all-day event, and everyone played a role in preparing the sheep. Traditionally, mutton ribs are grilled over an open fire and served with tortillas or fry bread, but this modern version uses the oven. This recipe calls for mutton ribs, but lamb ribs can also be used. I like to serve these with Navajo Tortillas (page 33) or Fry Bread (page 34).

Yield: 4 servings	Prep time: 15 minutes	Cook time: 1½ hours

2 pounds (about half a rack, or 910 g) mutton or lamb ribs

1 tablespoon extra-virgin olive oil

1 teaspoon salt

Navajo Tortillas (page 33) or Fry Bread (page 34), for serving

1. Preheat the oven to 350°F (180°C). Line a roasting pan or large baking dish with aluminum foil.

2. Prepare the mutton ribs by trimming any excess fat with a knife. This can be to your liking; I like to leave on 10 to 15 percent of the fat.

3. Place the ribs into the prepared roasting pan. Rub them with the olive oil and sprinkle with salt on both sides. Turn the ribs meat side up.

4. Cover the pan with foil and roast for 1 hour.

5. Remove the foil and raise the oven temperature to 425°F (220°C). Roast for another 30 minutes, until the top is dark brown and the internal temperature reads 170°F (77°C).

6. Remove the pan from the oven and let the ribs rest for 5 minutes. Then, slice the ribs with a chef's knife and tongs.

7. Serve immediately with tortillas or fry bread.

Dibé Yázhí Bitsį' Lees'áán Bił Yisdisí

Lamb Sandwich

If you ever ask a Navajo their favorite sandwich, they will almost always say a mutton sandwich. A mutton sandwich is a tortilla- or fry bread–wrapped sandwich that has roasted mutton and roasted Hatch green chile. In the western part of the Navajo Nation, it is also served with corn on the cob and a roasted potato. However, instead of the traditional mutton, I personally enjoy lamb, as the meat is a little more tender. The lamb is typically made on an outdoor grill, but this recipe uses a skillet.

Yield: 4 servings	Prep time: 10 minutes	Cook time: 42 minutes

1 pound (455 g) boneless lamb leg roast or lamb loin

½ teaspoon salt

2 teaspoons extra-virgin olive oil

4 Navajo Tortillas (page 33)

4 roasted mild or hot Hatch green chiles (see page 25), peeled and seeded

1. Prepare the lamb by trimming any excess fat with a knife. Cut the meat into ¼-inch (6 mm) slices. Dry with a paper towel, then sprinkle the salt on both sides of the meat. Set aside.

2. Warm a large pan or cast-iron skillet over medium-high heat for 5 minutes. Add the olive oil and warm it up for 5 minutes.

3. Add the mutton slices to the pan, but do not overcrowd it. There should be at least 1 inch (2.5 cm) between each slice. You may have to fry the slices in two batches. Let the meat cook untouched for 8 minutes, then flip over and cook the other side for an additional 8 minutes, until a brown crust is formed.

4. Add two to three slices of the mutton to each tortilla. Top with a green chile. Serve immediately.

Dah Díníilghaazh Bikáá' Ashjaa'í
Navajo Tacos

Navajo tacos are a modern staple in Navajo cuisine. It is not a traditional food, but an Indigenous dish that is referred to as an Indian taco. Each tribe has their own version of it. A Navajo taco is usually made on a thin, large fry bread topped with ground beef, chili beans, lettuce, tomatoes, onions, and cheese. Navajo tacos are usually served at large family gatherings and public events like powwows and Native markets. I like to serve Navajo tacos with fresh spinach instead of lettuce. Most Navajo tacos are eaten like an open-faced taco with a fork and a knife. However, some like to fold it in half, like a traditional taco. My preferred way is to tear the fry bread into bite-size pieces before adding the toppings. This makes it easier to eat.

Yield: 4 servings	Prep time: 15 minutes	Cook time: 8 hours 30 minutes
4 Navajo Fry Bread (page 34) 4 cups (513 g) Chili Beans (page 74) ½ cup to 1 cup (55 to 115 g) shredded cheddar or other sharp cheese ½ cup (65 g) diced (about ¼ inch, or 6 mm) red onion 2 cups (60 g) chopped fresh spinach ½ cup (90 g) diced (about ¼ inch, or 6 mm) tomatoes	Place each fry bread on a plate. To each fry bread, add 1 cup (171 g) chili beans, 2 to 4 tablespoons shredded cheese, 1 tablespoon diced onions, ½ cup (15 g) spinach, and 2 tablespoons tomatoes. Repeat for each taco. Serve warm.	

Atsị' Yik'ą́ Náneeskadí Bił Ałch'ị' Át'éhí

Navajo Burger

A Navajo burger is a traditional American hamburger patty served on a Navajo tortilla or fry bread. It is commonly served at the flea market or family cookouts. Typically, two hamburger patties are placed on one side of the tortilla or fry bread and then it is folded in half to make a sandwich. For this recipe, I made a few spicy additions, including New Mexico red chile powder in the hamburger and pepper jack cheese on top.

Yield: 2 to 4 servings	Prep time: 15 minutes	Cook time: 30 minutes

1 pound (455 g) ground beef

1 teaspoon garlic powder

1 teaspoon New Mexico red chile powder

1 teaspoon onion powder

1 teaspoon salt

1 teaspoon extra-virgin olive oil

1 medium yellow onion, cut into ¼-inch (6 mm) slices

4 slices pepper jack cheese

4 Navajo Tortillas (page 33)

4 leaves romaine lettuce

1 medium tomato, cut into ¼-inch (6 mm) slices

Ketchup, for serving (optional)

Mustard, for serving (optional)

1. Prepare the meat: In a medium bowl, mix the ground beef, garlic powder, red chile powder, onion powder, and ½ teaspoon of salt with your hands until evenly combined. Divide the hamburger mixture into four balls. Flatten each ball into a patty ¼ inch (6 mm) thick. Place the patties on a plate and set aside.

2. Prepare the grilled onions: In a medium pan over medium heat, warm up the olive oil for 5 minutes. Add the onions and remaining ½ teaspoon salt and cook for 6 to 8 minutes, stirring occasionally with a wooden spatula, until the onions are softened and slightly browned. Transfer the grilled onions to a medium bowl and set aside.

3. Cook the meat: Warm up a large nonstick pan or cast-iron skillet over medium heat for 5 minutes. Add the patties and cook for 5 minutes on each side, or until the meat reaches an internal temperature of 160°F (71°C). Add the cheese to each burger and remove from the heat.

4. Assemble the burgers: Place a tortilla on a plate, then place a hamburger patty on one side of the tortilla. Top with the grilled onions, lettuce, and tomato. Fold over the tortilla and serve with ketchup or mustard if desired. Enjoy!

Nímasii dóó Atsį' Yik'ąst'éhí
Potatoes and Ground Beef Bowl

Fried potatoes and ground beef made weekly appearances on the dinner table growing up. As an adult, it is one of my favorite comfort foods. Whenever this dish is made, it reminds me of shimá and shimásání and how they would slice the potatoes with a paring knife. A cutting board and chef's knife were rarely used. This quick and easy recipe pairs well with Navajo Tortillas (page 33), and while I grew up having this for dinner, it can be made for any meal. You can also make this into a breakfast burrito. Depending on the season, corn, squash, and green chile can be added.

Yield: 4 servings	Prep time: 10 minutes	Cook time: 25 minutes

4 medium russet potatoes

1 pound (455 g) ground beef

½ cup (65 g) diced (about ¼ inch, or 6 mm) white onion

½ teaspoon salt

½ teaspoon garlic powder

Navajo Tortillas (page 33), for serving

1. Peel and rinse the potatoes. Cut the potatoes into ¼-inch (6 mm) half-moon slices. Add the sliced potatoes to a colander and rinse with cold water for 1 minute. Set aside.

2. In a large pan over medium heat, cook the ground beef, breaking it into small crumbles with a spatula, for 8 to 10 minutes, until it is browned.

3. Turn off the heat. Drain all but 2 tablespoons or so of the grease in the pan and return the pan to the stove.

4. Add the onions to the pan and cook for 2 minutes over medium heat. Stir in the potatoes, salt, and garlic powder. Cover and cook for 15 to 18 minutes, stirring occasionally, until the potatoes are slightly soft and cooked through.

5. Serve in bowls with tortillas.

Naayízí, Naadą́ą́' dóó Azeed-ích'íí' Dootł'izhí Ak'ah Áłchx'íį́ dígo Bee Sit'éhí

Squash, Corn, and Green Chile Bowl

The three sisters (corn, beans, and squash) are not common to Navajo cuisine, admittedly, but the combination of squash, corn, and green chile is a modern classic. During the Navajo harvest season, there is always plentiful Navajo squash, Navajo corn, and freshly roasted green chiles. When I was younger, we had a garden, and this was my favorite meal to make with our harvest. Together it is one of the best combinations of food. I personally enjoy this with hot green chiles, but a mild green chile also pairs well for those who don't like super-spicy chiles. This is best served with Navajo Tortillas (page 33).

Yield: 4 servings	Prep time: 10 minutes	Cook time: 20 minutes

2 ears sweet corn

1 teaspoon extra-virgin olive oil

½ cup (65 g) diced (¼ inch, or 6 mm) yellow onion

4 garlic cloves, minced

½ teaspoon salt

1 medium yellow squash, sliced into ¼-inch half-moons

1 medium zucchini, sliced into ¼-inch half-moons

1 cup (150 g) diced (¼ inch, or 6 mm) roasted Hatch green chiles (see page 25)

Navajo Tortillas (page 33), for serving

1. Remove the kernels from the sweet corn with a chef's knife and set aside.

2. In a large nonstick pan over medium heat, warm up the olive oil for 3 minutes. Add the onions, garlic, and salt and cook for 3 minutes, until the onions are translucent.

3. Add the yellow squash and zucchini and cook for 5 minutes, until slightly softened.

4. Add the corn and the green chiles and cook for 15 minutes, until the vegetables are tender, stirring occasionally.

5. Serve in bowls with tortillas.

Naadą́'éłgai Tamale Atsı̨' Yik'ą́ dóó Azeedích'íiłchí'í bił

Navajo Tamales

These tamales incorporate traditional Navajo tamales with Mexican and Pueblo flavors. They are also fully wrapped in a corn husk, as opposed to a Mexican tamale, which is open at one end. These tamales are typically made year-round.

Yield: 10 to 11 servings	Prep time: 45 minutes	Cook time: 45 minutes

30 to 35 dried corn husks

6 medium (or 8 small) dried mild New Mexico red chiles

2 cups (480 ml) hot water

1 pound (455 g) ground beef

1 teaspoon salt

2 cups yellow sweet corn

1 teaspoon garlic powder

3 cups (390 g) white corn masa harina or instant white corn masa flour

2 tablespoons extra-virgin olive oil

2½ cups (600 ml) warm water or beef broth

1. Prepare the corn husks: Rinse the husks in warm water for 30 to 40 seconds to remove any debris. Place the rinsed husks in a large heat-safe bowl. Add hot water until all the husks are fully submerged. Set the corn husks aside to soak.

2. Prepare the dried chiles by rinsing each chile in warm water for 30 to 40 seconds. Remove and discard the stems and seeds. Add the chiles and the 2 cups (480 ml) hot water to a blender and let sit for 5 minutes. Blend on medium speed for 5 to 6 minutes, until the chiles have broken down into a smooth paste. Strain the sauce through a fine-mesh strainer into a medium bowl and set aside.

3. In a large pan over medium heat, cook the ground beef, breaking it into small crumbles with a spatula, for 8 to 10 minutes, until it is browned. Remove from the heat and drain the grease.

4. Return the pan to the stove over medium heat. Stir in the salt and corn and cook for 5 minutes, until the corn is warmed through and tender.

5. Stir the chile sauce and garlic powder into the ground beef mixture and cook for 5 minutes, until the sauce has thickened. Set aside.

6. Prepare the masa: In a medium bowl, mix together the masa harina and olive oil with your hands until fully combined. Slowly add the warm water, ½ cup (120 ml) at a time, and mix with your hands. The masa should be slightly thick but spreadable. If the dough is too thick, add an additional ¼ cup (60 ml) warm water.

7. Assemble the tamales: Take two corn husks with the waxy side facing up and overlap the two husks so that the widest parts are overlapped by 1 inch (2.5 cm) in the center. It should resemble a boat shape.

8. Scoop ⅓ cup (45 g) of the masa mixture into the middle of the overlapping husks. With your hands, spread and flatten the masa into a rectangle about 7 inches (18 cm) long and 5 inches (13 cm) wide. Add ¼ cup (56 g) of the meat filling in the center of the masa, then fold the husk lengthwise, aligning the sides of the husk together in order to seal the filling. Then fold each end of the corn husks to the center. Tie both flaps down with thin strips of the extra corn husks. Continue until all the filling is used, making 10 or 11 tamales.

9. In a 20-quart (19 L) tamale steamer (or stock pot; see page 16), add enough water so that it just touches the bottom of the steamer basket. Bring the water to a boil over medium-high heat. Once the water starts to boil, carefully add the tamales to the basket, standing them upright. Cover the pot and let cook for 45 minutes, until the masa easily pulls away from the husk.

10. Let the tamales cool for 10 to 15 minutes. Remove the outer husk and enjoy warm.

Dibé Yázhí Bitsį' Naadą́ą́' Yik'ą́ bił Meatballs Ályaaí
Lamb Meatballs

Ground lamb is not common to Navajo cuisine, but I often crave new ways to enjoy lamb. This recipe incorporates white cornmeal, a Navajo food staple. It acts like bread crumbs to provide more flavor and moisture to the meatballs. I like serving this with Sumac Berry Jam (page 119) and warm Blue Corn Flour Tortillas (page 45).

Yield: 25 meatballs	Prep time: 10 minutes	Cook time: 20 minutes

1 pound (455 g) ground lamb (85 percent lean)

¼ cup (45 g) white cornmeal

¼ cup (35 g) finely diced (⅛ inch, or 3 mm) sweet yellow onion

1 large egg

1 teaspoon garlic powder

¼ teaspoon dried thyme

½ teaspoon salt

½ teaspoon ground black pepper

4 teaspoons extra-virgin olive oil

Sumac Berry Jam (page 119), for serving

Blue Corn Flour Tortillas (page 45), for serving

1. In a medium bowl, mix together the ground lamb, cornmeal, onion, egg, garlic powder, thyme, salt, and pepper until combined. Assemble the meatballs by portioning out a tablespoon of meat and rolling it into a ball with your hands. Set the ball on a large plate and repeat until all balls are formed, about twenty-five meatballs.

2. In a large nonstick pan over medium heat, warm up the olive oil for 5 minutes. Add the meatballs and cook uncovered for 5 minutes. With tongs, flip the meatballs over and cook for another 5 minutes. Stir the meatballs with a wooden spoon and cook for another 5 minutes, covered, until all sides are browned and the internal temperature reaches 145°F (63°C).

3. Serve warm with sumac berry jam and Navajo tortillas.

Náneeskadí Téél Atsį' dóó Saucełchí'í bił

Navajo Pizza

This is a modern recipe that uses Navajo tortillas as a pizza crust to make personal pepperoni pizzas. It is fun to make with your little ones. My husband shared this recipe as a childhood favorite that he made when he was younger while staying at his grandma's house during the summer on the Navajo Nation. He would crave modern flavors and make pizzas using leftover tortillas and whatever toppings he would find. I really enjoy making these with my family because they are quick and easy. We like topping ours with pepperoni, but use your favorite pizza toppings.

Yield: 16 slices	Prep time: 5 minutes	Cook time: 10 minutes

4 Navajo Tortillas (page 33)

1 cup (240 ml) red pasta sauce

1 cup (112 g) Italian blended shredded cheese

½ cup (65 g) sliced pepperoni

1. Place a rack in the middle of the oven and preheat the oven to 400°F (200°C). Line a sheet pan with aluminum foil.

2. Assemble the pizzas: Place the tortillas onto the prepared sheet pan and spread ¼ cup (60 ml) of pasta sauce on each tortilla with a spoon. Add ¼ cup (28 g) of shredded cheese to each tortilla. Evenly spread the pepperoni over the top.

3. Bake for 8 to 10 minutes, until the cheese is melted and the pepperoni is slightly toasted.

4. Let cool and slice each tortilla into 4 pieces with a pizza cutter.

Naa'ołí Azeedích'íí' Naadą́ą́' Bááhkáa'í

Chili Bean Cornmeal Casserole

Brown tepary beans are commonly used by the local tribes, the Akimel O'odham and the Toho O'odham, here in Phoenix, Arizona, where I live. Tepary beans are packed with flavor and can be eaten alone as a soup or stew. Whenever I make beans, I sometimes make too many. I like making this casserole with leftover tepary beans or 3 cups (513 g) of Chili Beans (page 74).

Yield: 9 servings	Prep time: 20 minutes, plus overnight soaking of beans	Cook time: 4 to 8 hours

2 cups (370 g) dried brown tepary beans

1 teaspoon garlic powder

½ teaspoon onion powder

½ cup (75 g) chopped roasted Hatch green chiles (see page 25)

½ cup (90 g) yellow cornmeal

½ cup (60 g) all-purpose flour

2 tablespoons sugar

1 teaspoon baking powder

¼ teaspoon salt

1 large egg

½ cup (120 ml) milk

2 tablespoons vegetable oil

1. Prepare the beans by rinsing them with cold water for 2 minutes to remove any debris. Add the beans to a medium bowl and cover with water completely so that there are 3 to 4 inches (8 to 10 cm) of water above the beans. Cover and let sit overnight.

2. The next day, drain and rinse the beans with cold water and set aside.

3. In a 7- to 10-quart (6 to 9 L) slow cooker, stir together the beans, 8 cups (1.9 L) of water, the garlic powder, onion powder, and green chiles. Cook on high for 4 to 5 hours or on low for 6 to 8 hours, until the beans are tender.

4. When the beans are finished cooking, turn the slow cooker to its lowest setting.

5. Place a rack in the middle of the oven and preheat the oven to 350°F (180°C).

6. Add 3 cups (465 g) of the cooked beans to an 9-inch (23 cm) square baking dish. You don't want to include too much of the liquid. Set aside.

7. Prepare the cornmeal batter: In a medium bowl, whisk together the cornmeal, flour, sugar, baking powder, and salt until combined.

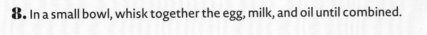

8. In a small bowl, whisk together the egg, milk, and oil until combined.

9. Add the wet ingredients to the dry ingredients and whisk together until the batter is smooth.

10. Evenly pour the cornmeal batter on top of the beans. With a spoon or spatula, carefully spread the batter across the beans. Please note that the batter will not reach the sides of the dish.

11. Bake for 20 to 25 minutes, until the corn bread starts to turn golden on top and a toothpick inserted in the middle of the corn bread comes out clean.

12. Cut the casserole into nine equal squares and enjoy warm.

Íyisí Daadą́ągo Daabiłígíí
SIDES & PANTRY STAPLES

No meal is complete without a delicious side to brighten it. When it comes to Navajo cuisine, a lot of the main dishes are very hearty, and a good side will help balance out the meal. In this chapter you will learn how to make pantry staples like Sumac Berry Jam (page 119) and Berry Compote (page 123). There are also fresh sides like Blue Corn Bread Stuffing (page 111), Roasted Pumpkin (page 112), Three Sisters Pasta Salad (page 115), Sumac Berry Fruit Salad (page 116), and Corn Salsa (page 124).

Naadą́ą́' Dootł'izhí Bááhtaas'éí
Blue Corn Bread Stuffing

Blue corn bread stuffing incorporates the traditional flavors of Navajo blue corn bread in a common American dish. I like making this during the holidays, especially around Thanksgiving. It is an easy dish to bring to a holiday potluck.

Yield: 8 to 10 servings	Prep time: 20 minutes	Cook time: 1 hour

Blue Corn Bread (page 41)

4 tablespoons extra-virgin olive oil

2 teaspoons salt

2 teaspoons ground black pepper

½ cup (65 g) diced (about ¼ inch, or 6 mm) yellow onion

1 cup (140 g) diced (about ¼ inch, or 6 mm) carrots

1 cup (100 g) diced (about ¼ inch, or 6 mm) celery

6 fresh sage leaves, chopped

1 teaspoon dried parsley

1 teaspoon dried thyme

1 teaspoon garlic powder

1 to 2 cups (240 to 480 ml) vegetable broth

1. Place a rack in the middle of the oven and preheat the oven to 400°F (200°C). Line a sheet pan with parchment paper.

2. Slice the corn bread into 1-inch (2.5 cm) cubes and transfer it to the prepared sheet pan. Drizzle with 2 tablespoons of the olive oil and sprinkle with 1 teaspoon of the salt and 1 teaspoon of the pepper. Mix lightly with your hands or tongs.

3. Bake for 6 to 8 minutes, until golden brown. Flip the corn bread over with tongs and bake for another 6 to 8 minutes. Remove from the oven and let cool.

4. Reduce the oven temperature to 350°F (180°C).

5. In a medium pan or cast-iron skillet over medium heat, warm up the remaining 2 tablespoons olive oil for 5 minutes. Add the onions and cook for 5 to 6 minutes, until translucent. Add the carrots, celery, sage, parsley, thyme, garlic powder, remaining 1 teaspoon salt, and remaining 1 teaspoon pepper and cook, covered, for 8 to 10 minutes, until the carrots are slightly softened.

6. In a large 9 by 13-inch baking dish (23 by 33 cm), combine the corn bread and cooked vegetables. Lightly toss with tongs. Then slowly add in the broth, ½ cup (120 ml) at a time, and lightly toss together. The corn bread should be moistened, not completely drenched.

7. Bake for 20 to 25 minutes, until the corn bread starts to turn a golden brown. Serve warm.

Naayízí
Roasted Pumpkin

This easy recipe incorporates two cooking methods to bring out the flavors of roasted pumpkin. In Navajo cuisine, pumpkins and large squashes are commonly boiled. Boiling makes the pumpkin very soft and tender, but sometimes it can make it too watery. To firm up the pumpkin, I like to roast it after it is boiled. Together this makes for the softest and most delicious pumpkin. For this recipe I enjoy adding butter with brown sugar or maple sugar on top. For a savory flavor, you can drizzle some olive oil and sprinkle on red chile powder before roasting.

Yield: 4 servings	Prep time: 10 minutes	Cook time: 40 minutes

1 medium to large pie (sugar) pumpkin

¼ cup (55 g) salted butter, thinly sliced

¼ cup (55 g) brown sugar or maple sugar

1. With a chef's knife, cut the pumpkin in half and remove the seeds. Slice the pumpkin halves into 2- to 3-inch (5 to 8 cm) wedges.

2. In a large pot, combine the wedges and enough water so that the pumpkin is fully submerged. Bring to a boil over medium-high heat and let boil for 15 to 20 minutes, until the pumpkin is softened. Transfer the boiled pumpkin to a paper towel–lined plate.

3. Preheat the oven to 425°F (220°C). Line a sheet pan with aluminum foil.

4. Place the pumpkin wedges skin side down on the prepared sheet pan. Add a slice of butter to each wedge. Evenly sprinkle the brown sugar on top. Bake for 15 to 20 minutes, until the sugar mixture melts into the pumpkin. Serve warm.

Táá' Ałdeezhí Ch'il Ałtaas'éí
Three Sisters Pasta Salad

This is a modern recipe that incorporates acorn squash, sweet corn, and pinto beans to make a refreshing pasta salad with a maple vinaigrette. It's a fun dish to bring to a family cookout or potluck.

Yield: 6 servings	Prep time: 20 minutes	Cook time: 30 minutes, plus 30 minutes of refrigeration

PASTA SALAD

1 small acorn squash

2 ears yellow or white sweet corn

1 can (15.5 ounces, or 439 g) pinto beans

2 cups (200 g) rotini pasta

¼ cup extra-virgin olive oil

½ teaspoon salt

1 cup (35 g) spring mix salad

VINAIGRETTE

⅓ cup (80 ml) apple cider vinegar

1 tablespoon olive oil

3 tablespoons maple syrup

¼ teaspoon salt

¼ teaspoon ground black pepper

1. With a chef's knife, cut the acorn squash in half and remove the seeds. Cut the squash into 1-inch (2.5 cm) cubes and set aside.

2. Prepare the sweet corn by removing the husks and cutting off all the kernels. Set aside.

3. Prepare the pinto beans by draining and rinsing the beans twice. Set aside.

4. Prepare the pasta: Bring 4 cups (960 ml) of water to a boil over medium-high heat. Add the pasta and cook for 10 minutes, just past al dente. Drain and rinse with cold water until the pasta is cool.

5. In a large pan over medium heat, warm up the olive oil for 5 minutes. Add the squash, cover, and cook for 6 to 8 minutes, until slightly softened. Add the corn and salt. Cover and cook for an additional 5 minutes, until the corn is tender. Remove from the heat and let cool completely.

6. Prepare the vinaigrette: In a small bowl, whisk together the vinegar, olive oil, maple syrup, salt, and pepper for 2 minutes.

7. In a large bowl, combine the pasta, squash and corn mixture, beans, spring mix, and dressing and mix together with tongs until thoroughly combined.

8. Refrigerate for at least 30 minutes. Serve cold.

Aneest'e' Ałtaas'éí Chiiłchin Bitoo' Bik'isziidí
Sumac Berry Fruit Salad

Sumac berry dressing is a revitalized recipe that incorporates classic and modern Navajo flavors in a fresh fruit salad. Ground sumac berries were traditionally added to boiled or mashed fruits for a sweet-tart treat in the olden days. It is best to wait to add the sumac dressing until you are about to serve the salad or it will start to draw out the juices of the fruit.

Yield: 8 to 10 servings	Prep time: 15 minutes

DRESSING

¼ cup (60 ml) honey

1 teaspoon fresh lemon juice

1 teaspoon ground sumac berries

SALAD

2 cups (330 g) strawberries, cut into ¼-inch (6 mm) slices

2 cups (290 g) blueberries

2 cups (300 g) green or purple grapes, halved

2 medium bananas, cut into ¼-inch (6 mm) slices

1. Prepare the dressing: In a small bowl, whisk together the honey, lemon juice, and ground sumac berries.

2. Prepare the salad: In a medium bowl, stir together the strawberries, blueberries, grapes, and bananas.

3. Add the dressing and stir until the salad is evenly coated. Serve immediately.

Chiiłchin Jelii
Sumac Berry Jam

Sumac berry jam is a modern way to use chiiłchin, or ground sumac berries, which are different from the ground sumac berries that may be found in grocery stores and Mediterranean markets. This jam is a beautiful red color that brightens up any dish and pairs well with Biscuits (page 37) and Lamb Meatballs (page 103). Ground sumac berries can be found at local flea markets and trading posts on the Navajo Nation.

Yield: 1 cup (240 ml)	Prep time: 5 minutes	Cook time: 30 minutes

1 tablespoon ground sumac berries

1 cup (200 g) sugar

1 teaspoon fresh lemon juice

1½ teaspoons pectin

1. In a medium saucepan, whisk together 2 cups (480 ml) of water and the ground sumac berries. Bring to a boil over medium heat and let boil for 10 minutes, until the mixture turns a light red color.

2. Stir in the sugar and boil for 5 minutes.

3. Stir in the lemon juice and pectin. Bring the mixture back up to a boil and then boil for 10 to 15 minutes, until the mixture reads 217° to 220°F (103° to 104°C) on a candy thermometer or the mixture reduces by half and has a gel-like consistency. Remove from the heat and let cool for 10 minutes.

4. Transfer the jam to a heat-safe container and let it cool completely.

5. Refrigerate overnight before using. The jam can be stored in the refrigerator for 2 weeks.

Neeshchx'íí' Mandigíiya
Piñon Nut Butter

This nut butter uses piñons, or pine nuts, that are usually harvested in the late summer. Nut butters were more common in the olden days. A lot of time and effort goes into picking piñons, but growing up, it was a fun way to spend the day with family. They are an expensive nut, so this is made sparingly. You can use freshly harvested piñons or raw pine nuts from the grocery store. Piñon nut butter can be used to make Piñon Lattes (page 158), or you can spread it on Navajo Tortillas (page 33) for a delicious snack.

Yield: ½ cup (120 ml)	Cook time: 8 minutes

½ cup (65 g) shelled raw pine nuts

2 teaspoons canola oil

1 teaspoon honey

1. Warm up a small pan over medium heat for 5 minutes. Add the pine nuts and toast for 2 to 3 minutes, until they turn golden brown. Stir continuously so they do not overtoast. Remove the nuts from the pan and let them cool for 10 minutes.

2. In a mini food processor, add the toasted pine nuts, oil, and honey and blend on high for 3 to 5 minutes, until the mixture is smooth and creamy. Scrape down the sides with a spatula to make sure all the nuts are pureed.

Dahwoozh dóó Blueberries Bitoo'kání

Berry Compote

Berry compote is not a traditional Navajo recipe, but it's common practice in Native American cooking to make juice out of fruits or mash them into a puree. I use compote a lot in my cooking as a replacement for syrups. Depending on the season, you can switch out the fruits. I like topping Blue Corn Pancakes (page 61) and Sweet Blue Corn Tamales (page 144) with warm berry compote. It adds not only some extra sweetness but also a vibrant color.

Yield: 1 cup (240 ml)	Prep time: 5 minutes	Cook time: 15 minutes
1 cup (145 g) blueberries 1 cup (165 g) diced (about ¼ inch, or 6 mm) strawberries 3 tablespoons sugar	In a small saucepan, stir together the blueberries, strawberries, sugar, and ½ cup (120 ml) of water. Bring to a boil on medium heat. Let boil for 5 minutes, then reduce the heat to low and simmer for 10 minutes, until thickened. Serve immediately.	

Naadą́'áłtsóí Sit'é Azeedích'íí' Bił Tanaashgiizhí

Corn Salsa

When I was growing up in the Southwest, salsas were a common condiment on the dining table. Typically, the salsas I ate as a child were heavily tomato based, but for this recipe, the roasted corn is the star. I like making this in the summertime to add some fresh flavors.

Yield: 3 to 4 cups (435 to 580 g)	Prep time: 15 minutes	Cook time: 10 minutes

1 teaspoon extra-virgin olive oil

3 ears yellow sweet corn, shucked

2 tablespoons apple cider vinegar

½ teaspoon paprika

1 tablespoon garlic powder

¼ teaspoon salt

¼ teaspoon ground black pepper

1 red bell pepper, diced into ¼-inch (6 mm) pieces

2 large Roma tomatoes, diced into ¼-inch (6 mm) pieces

½ small red onion, diced into ¼-inch (6 mm) pieces

2 to 4 large jalapeños (depending on desired spice level), diced into ¼-inch (6 mm) pieces

¼ cup (10 g) chopped fresh cilantro

1. In a large pan or cast-iron skillet over medium-high heat, warm up the olive oil for 5 minutes. Add the corn and cook for 10 minutes, turning every 2 minutes, so that each side is charred. Let the corn cool for 10 minutes.

2. In a small bowl, whisk together the vinegar, paprika, garlic powder, salt, and pepper until combined.

3. With a chef's knife, cut the kernels off the corn and transfer to a medium bowl.

4. Add the bell pepper, tomatoes, onion, jalapeños, and cilantro to the same bowl and mix together until evenly combined.

5. Pour in the vinegar mixture and toss to combine.

6. Refrigerate for at least 30 minutes and serve with some tortilla chips.

Likání Ádaat'éhígíí
DESSERTS

This is probably my favorite chapter of this book because it was the catalyst to my starting *The Fancy Navajo*. When I was growing up, there weren't many desserts in Navajo cuisine other than traditional corn recipes. As a way to bridge traditional and modern flavors these are some of my favorite recipes that highlight Navajo ingredients. These desserts have the perfect amount of sweetness and, most importantly, they don't take too long to make.

Naadą́ą́' Dootł'izhí Bááhkání Yázhí

Blue Corn Cupcakes

This is one of the most popular recipes on my food blog, *The Fancy Navajo*, and it was the catalyst to my adventures of finding new ways to use traditional Navajo ingredients in contemporary foods. I wanted a way to celebrate reaching one thousand followers on my Instagram back in 2017. Now I can't believe we are over fifty thousand followers across all my social media channels as of 2023!

When I was growing up, there weren't many American-style desserts in Navajo cuisine. Noticing how I had a lot of blue cornmeal in my pantry, I decided to make blue corn cupcakes with vanilla buttercream and piñon sprinkles. They were an absolute hit! This recipe is an updated version of the original.

Yield: 12 cupcakes	Prep time: 25 minutes	Bake time: 15 to 18 minutes

CUPCAKES

¾ cup (135 g) roasted blue cornmeal (see page 27)

¾ cup (90 g) all-purpose flour

1 teaspoon baking powder

½ teaspoon juniper ash (see page 23)

¼ teaspoon salt

½ cup (115 g) unsalted butter, melted and cooled

¼ cup (50 g) granulated sugar

2 large eggs

¾ cup (180 ml) milk

1 tablespoon vanilla extract

1. Place a rack in the middle of the oven and preheat the oven to 350°F (180°C). Line a cupcake pan with cupcake liners.

2. Prepare the cupcakes: Sift the blue cornmeal through a fine-mesh strainer into a medium bowl. Discard any debris left in the strainer.

3. Add the flour, baking powder, juniper ash, and salt and whisk together. Set aside.

4. In another medium bowl, whisk together the melted butter, granulated sugar, and eggs until combined. Whisk in the milk and vanilla.

5. Slowly whisk the dry ingredients into the wet ingredients until combined.

6. Using a spoon or ice cream scoop, fill the cupcake liners two-thirds of the way full with the cupcake batter.

7. Bake for 15 to 18 minutes, until a toothpick inserted in the center comes out clean. Let cool completely.

VANILLA BUTTERCREAM FROSTING

½ cup (115 g) unsalted butter, at room temperature

2 teaspoons vanilla extract

¼ teaspoon salt

3 cups (360 g) powdered sugar

2 to 4 tablespoons heavy cream

Piñons (pine nuts), for topping (optional)

8. Prepare the frosting: In a large bowl, add the butter, vanilla, and salt. Using an electric hand mixer (you can also use a stand mixer fitted with the paddle attachment), mix on medium speed for 2 minutes, until light and fluffy. Slowly incorporate the powdered sugar, about ½ cup (60 g) at a time, until fully combined.

9. Add 2 tablespoons of the cream and mix on low speed until combined. If the frosting is too thick or not spreadable, add an additional tablespoon of cream. Once the right consistency is achieved, mix on high speed for 1 minute.

10. Frost the cupcakes either with a spatula or using a piping bag. Sprinkle the tops with piñons, if desired.

Tin Ta'neesk'áník'ǫzhí Chiiłchin Yik'ání Bił
Piccadilly

Piccadilly is a modern dessert that has gained popularity in recent years on the Navajo Nation. If you have never heard of it, it's a syrupy shaved iced dessert that is topped with chopped pickles and sprinkled with Kool-Aid powder. It is typically sold at local flea markets and urban Native markets. The sweet and sour flavors may seem off-putting, but they go well together.

The first time I tried this dessert, I couldn't help but notice the sprinkled Kool-Aid powder was similar to the flavor of ground sumac berries, which are naturally lemony and tart. This recipe is a reimagined version of piccadilly that uses traditional Navajo sumac berries (see page 17) and a homemade berry syrup that is perfect for the summertime.

Yield: 4 servings	Prep time: 15 minutes	Cook time: 8 minutes

1 cup (145 g) blueberries

¼ cup (50 g) sugar

4 cups (870 g) shaved or finely crushed ice

¼ cup (25 g) diced (¼ inch, or 6 mm) pickles

1 teaspoon ground sumac berries

1. In a small saucepan, combine the blueberries, 1 cup (240 ml) of water, and the sugar. Bring the mixture to a boil over medium heat, then reduce the heat to medium-low and simmer for 5 to 8 minutes, until the mixture starts to thicken and the water has reduced to half its volume.

2. Remove the pan from the heat and let the berry sauce cool completely, 15 to 20 minutes. Once cooled, transfer to a blender and blend on high speed for 2 to 3 minutes, until it reaches a smooth consistency. Pour the berry sauce into a small bowl with a lid and store in the refrigerator until ready to use. This can be made 1 to 2 days in advance.

3. Add a cup of shaved ice to four small bowls. Drizzle with 3 to 4 tablespoons of the berry sauce, so that the ice is completely covered. Top with 1 to 2 teaspoons of the pickles and sprinkle with ¼ teaspoon of the ground sumac berries. Serve immediately.

'Alkaad
Navajo Sweet Corn Cake

Navajo sweet corn cake, or 'alkaan/'alkaad, is a cake made of white cornmeal, sugar, and raisins that is traditionally baked in corn husks in the ground. This is one of the first cakes that a young Navajo woman learns how to make. It is commonly made at a kinaaldá, a traditional Navajo puberty ceremony that celebrates Navajo womanhood. The cake is large and takes days to prepare. This is a smaller, at-home version that uses cranberries instead of raisins and can be eaten year-round.

Yield: 9 servings	Prep time: 15 minutes	Cook time: 1 hour 30 minutes

10 to 15 corn husks

3 cups (540 g) white cornmeal

⅓ cup (75 g) brown sugar

1 cup (140 g) dried cranberries

Navajo Coffee/Corn Creamer (page 161), optional

1. Place a rack in the middle of the oven and preheat the oven to 375°F (190°C).

2. Prepare the corn husks: Rinse the husks in warm water for 30 to 40 seconds to remove any debris. Place the cleaned corn husks in a large heat-safe bowl. Add hot water until all the husks are fully submerged. Set the corn husks aside to soak.

3. In a large pot over medium heat, whisk together the cornmeal and 4 cups (960 ml) of water. Add the water slowly, ½ cup (120 ml) at a time, and whisk continuously until all the water is added. This is to prevent lumps from forming.

4. Bring the mixture to a gentle boil, stirring constantly. Add the brown sugar and mix together until combined. Once the mixture reaches a boil, remove the pot from the heat and stir in the cranberries. Set aside. The mixture will be a really thick but spreadable mush.

5. Line the bottom and sides of an 8-inch (20 cm) square baking dish with the softened corn husks. The coarse side of the husks should face outward, lining the pan, and the waxy part should be inward, facing up. Overlap them so that the cornmeal mixture will not leak out. At least two large corn husks will be needed for each side of the pan, for a total of eight. If the corn husks are small, more may be needed.

6. Scoop the batter into the lined pan and evenly spread it so that it reaches all the edges of the pan.

7. Fold the corn husks on top of the cornmeal mixture so that it is fully wrapped. Add extra husks to the top if needed. Press down on the batter lightly with your hands to fill the corners. Cover with aluminum foil.

8. Bake for 1 hour. Remove the aluminum foil and then continue to bake at 425°F (220°C) for 25 to 30 minutes. The cake will be done when the center is firm and a toothpick inserted into the center comes out clean. Let the cake cool for at least 15 minutes.

9. Cut the cake with the husks on, but remove them before eating. Enjoy with a cup of coffee with creamer.

Chiiłchin Bááh Dá'áka'í
Sumac Berry Sugar Cookies

This is a modern recipe that incorporates the flavors of sumac and Navajo white corn. They pair well, giving the cookies a slight lemon/tart flavor. I like gifting these cookies to family and friends during the holidays. You can also make fun shapes. Serve with Navajo Tea (page 149) to have a fancy Navajo tea party.

Yield: 16 cookies	Prep time: 25 minutes	Cook time: 24 minutes

1 cup (120 g) all-purpose flour

1¼ cups (225 g) white cornmeal

½ teaspoon baking soda

½ teaspoon baking powder

¼ teaspoon salt

½ cup (115 g) cold unsalted butter

¾ cup (150 g) sugar

2 large eggs

2 teaspoons ground sumac berries

Navajo Tea (page 149), for serving

1. Place a rack in the middle of the oven and preheat the oven to 350°F (180°C). Line two sheet pans with parchment paper.

2. In a large bowl, whisk together the flour, cornmeal, baking soda, baking powder, and salt until combined.

3. In a separate large bowl, combine the butter and sugar. With an electric hand mixer (you can also use a stand mixer fitted with the paddle attachment), beat the butter and sugar for 4 minutes on medium-high speed, until light and fluffy. Then add the eggs and ground sumac berries and mix on medium speed for 2 minutes, until thoroughly combined.

4. Slowly add the dry ingredients on low speed and mix until combined.

5. Flour a clean surface and a rolling pin. Roll out the cookie dough to a ¼-inch (6 mm) thickness. With a 3-inch (8 cm) round cookie cutter, cut out the cookie shapes. Place them on the prepared sheet pan 2 inches (5 cm) apart. Eight cookies should fit on one pan.

6. Bake one pan of cookies for 10 to 12 minutes, until the edges of the cookies start to turn brown. Let cool for 2 minutes before removing from the sheet pan. Transfer to a rack to cool completely.

Naayízí Bááh Dá'áka'í
Maple Pumpkin Cookies

Baked goods are commonly sold at the flea market on the Navajo Nation, and cookies are one of my favorite items to pick up. Around the fall, soft pumpkin cookies are quite commonly made by the Pueblo tribes. This recipe reminds me of those cookies, but with a few fancy additions, like Indigenous maple sugar, which adds more flavor. I enjoy these with a cream cheese drizzle.

Yield: 12 cookies	Prep time: 20 minutes	Cook time: 15 minutes

COOKIES

½ cup (115 g) unsalted butter, softened

¾ cup maple sugar (110 g)

¼ cup brown sugar (55 g)

1 large egg

½ teaspoon baking soda

¼ teaspoon salt

1 teaspoon vanilla extract

½ cup (113 g) pumpkin puree

¼ teaspoon pumpkin pie spice

1½ cups (180 g) all-purpose flour

DRIZZLE

¼ cup (60 g) cream cheese, softened

¼ cup (30 g) powdered sugar

4 tablespoons milk

1. Place a rack in the middle of the oven and preheat the oven to 350°F (180°C). Line a sheet pan with parchment paper.

2. In the bowl of a stand mixer fitted with the paddle attachment, combine the butter, maple sugar, and brown sugar. Mix on high speed for 3 to 4 minutes (you can also use an electric hand mixer and a large bowl), until light and fluffy.

3. Add the egg, baking soda, salt, vanilla, pumpkin puree, and pumpkin pie spice and mix on medium speed for 2 to 3 minutes, until all the ingredients are combined.

4. Mix in the flour, ½ cup (60 g) at a time, until incorporated. The cookie dough will be light and fluffy.

5. Scoop the cookie batter, 1 tablespoon at a time, onto the prepared sheet pan, placing the cookies at least 2 inches (5 cm) apart.

6. Bake for 12 to 15 minutes, until the tops of the cookies are slightly brown. Let cool completely on the pan, at least 15 minutes.

7. Prepare the cream cheese drizzle: In a medium bowl, whisk together the cream cheese, powdered sugar, and 2 tablespoons of the milk until fully combined. If the drizzle is too thick, add the remaining 2 tablespoons milk.

8. Frost the cooled cookies, either with a piping bag or a spatula.

Dahistin
Navajo Ice Cream

Navajo ice cream, or dahistin, is a traditional Navajo way of making ice cream using blue cornmeal. Instead of using a freezer, the mush was placed in a dish on the roof to freeze overnight. It was then cut into squares and enjoyed in the morning. Traditionally it was made with water, blue cornmeal, and sugar or fresh fruit purees, making it more of a corn ice. This is a contemporary version of that recipe. I've added coconut milk, which helps give it more of an ice cream texture. If you live somewhere cold, this would be fun dessert to make with your children by letting it freeze outside.

Yield: 6 to 8 servings	Prep time: 5 minutes	Cook time: 15 minutes, plus freezing for 4 hours

1 cup (180 g) roasted blue cornmeal (see page 27)

1 can (13.5 ounces, or 400 ml) coconut milk

1 teaspoon juniper ash (see page 23)

1 teaspoon vanilla extract

¼ cup (50 g) sugar

1. In a medium bowl, whisk together the cornmeal and 1 cup (240 ml) of water until combined. Set aside.

2. In a medium saucepan over medium heat, whisk together the coconut milk and 1 cup (240 ml) of water. Bring the mixture to a boil and let it boil for 6 to 8 minutes.

3. Reduce the heat to medium-low. Whisk in the juniper ash, then let boil for 1 minute.

4. Whisk in the vanilla and sugar, then let boil for 2 minutes.

5. Slowly pour the blue corn mixture into the saucepan and mix together until combined. Let the mixture come back to a boil and boil for 5 minutes, stirring continuously. Remove from the heat and let it cool for at least 15 minutes.

6. Line an 8-inch (20 cm) square pan with parchment paper, then pour the blue corn mixture into the pan. Place the pan in the freezer overnight, or until the mixture is frozen solid, 4 to 6 hours.

7. Remove the ice cream and let it sit out for 10 to 15 minutes. Then slice into squares or scoop with an ice cream scoop. Serve immediately.

Naadą́ą́' Dootł'izhí Dahwoozh Bááhłkání

Blue Corn Strawberry Shortcakes

Strawberry shortcakes are a popular dessert on the Navajo reservation and can be found at the flea market. They're a fun treat to have on a summer day, and the colors always make me smile. This is a slightly healthier version made with blue cornmeal, a fresh strawberry filling with ground sumac berries, and homemade whipped cream.

Yield: 8 servings	Prep time: 15 minutes	Cook time: 18 minutes

BLUE CORN SHORTCAKES

1 cup (180 g) roasted blue cornmeal (see page 27)

1 cup (120 g) all-purpose flour

¼ cup (50 g) granulated sugar

2½ teaspoons baking powder

1 teaspoon juniper ash (see page 23)

½ teaspoon salt

1½ cups (360 ml) heavy cream

1 teaspoon vanilla extract

½ teaspoon organic cane sugar

STRAWBERRY FILLING

4 cups (660 g) strawberries, cut into ¼-inch (6 mm) slices or cubes

1 to 2 tablespoons granulated sugar, to taste

1 teaspoon ground sumac berries

1. Place a rack in the middle of the oven and preheat the oven to 425°F (220°C). Line a sheet pan with parchment paper.

2. Prepare the shortcakes: In a medium bowl, whisk together the cornmeal, flour, granulated sugar, baking powder, juniper ash, and salt until fully combined.

3. Pour in the cream and vanilla. With your hands or a wooden spoon, mix until all the dry ingredients are incorporated, forming a large ball of dough. Do not overmix or knead the dough. It should be slightly sticky.

4. Divide the dough into eight equal pieces. Roll each piece into a ball and flatten slightly to ½ to ¾-inch (1 to 2 cm) thick. Place each dough ball onto the prepared sheet pan and sprinkle with cane sugar.

5. Bake for 15 to 18 minutes, until the tops are lightly brown. Let cool completely, at least 10 minutes.

6. Prepare the strawberry filling: In a medium bowl, stir together the strawberries, sugar, and ground sumac berries. Set aside.

7. Prepare the whipped cream: In a blender or stand mixer fitted with the whisk attachment, combine the cream, vanilla, and powdered sugar. Mix on high speed for 3 to 4 minutes, until the mixture forms medium peaks. Transfer to a medium bowl with a lid and refrigerate until ready to use.

WHIPPED CREAM

2 cups (480 ml) heavy cream

1 teaspoon vanilla extract

1 teaspoon powdered sugar

Navajo Tea (page 149),
for serving

8. Assemble the shortcakes by slicing the shortcake in half and layering with strawberry filling and whipped cream to your liking. I like to add about 2 tablespoons of strawberry filling, then 2 to 3 tablespoons of whipped cream, and top with the shortcake. Then I top with another tablespoon each of strawberry filling and whipped cream.

9. Serve with Navajo tea.

Chiiłchin Yogurt Tiní
Sumac and Strawberry Greek Yogurt Ice Pops

This is a modern Navajo recipe that uses ground sumac berries, strawberries, honey, and Greek yogurt to make a refreshing, tart dessert. The sumac and strawberry complement each other so well. This recipe is one of my daughter's favorite treats. You can also use this as a base for a yogurt parfait and top with Corn Granola (page 58).

Yield: 6 servings	Prep time: 10 minutes, plus freezing for 6 hours
½ cup (85 g) diced (¼ inch, or 6 mm) strawberries 2 teaspoons ground sumac berries 1 tablespoon honey 1¾ cups (410 g) vanilla Greek yogurt	**1.** In a medium bowl, mix together the strawberries, ground sumac berries, and honey with a large spoon. Let the mixture sit for 5 minutes. **2.** Add the yogurt to the berry mixture and mix together. **3.** With a small spoon, fill the ice pop molds with the yogurt mixture until it fully reaches the top. Then top with the ice pop handles. **4.** Freeze for at least 6 hours or overnight, until the ice pops are set. **5.** To remove the ice pops from the molds, dip the bottom half of the mold in warm water for at least 1 minute, until the ice pop releases easily. Serve immediately.

Naadą́ą́' Dootł'izhí Tamaliiłkání
Sweet Blue Corn Tamales

Typically, these sweet blue corn tamales are made into mini tamales and are more popular among Navajo elders.

Yield: 11 mini tamales	Prep time: 30 minutes	Cook time: 30 minutes

15 dried corn husks

1 teaspoon juniper ash (see page 23)

1½ cups (270 g) roasted blue cornmeal (see page 27)

¼ cup (55 g) brown sugar

Berry Compote (page 123; optional)

1. Prepare the corn husks: Rinse the husks in warm water for 30 to 40 seconds to remove any debris. Place the rinsed husks in a large heat-safe bowl. Add warm water until all the husks are fully submerged. Set the corn husks aside to soak.

2. Prepare the filling: In a medium saucepan, whisk together the juniper ash and 1 cup (240 ml) of water. Bring to a boil over medium-high heat. Boil for 5 minutes and turn off the heat.

3. Add ½ cup (90 g) of the cornmeal to the saucepan and mix with a wooden spoon until combined. Repeat this process, ½ cup (90 g) at a time, until all the cornmeal is added. A thick dough will start to form.

4. Transfer the dough to a medium bowl. Add ¼ cup (60 ml) of water and mix into the dough with your hands for 2 minutes.

5. Add the brown sugar and mix until fully combined. Cover the dough and set aside.

6. Fill a large pot halfway with water and cover with a lid. Bring the water to a boil over medium heat.

7. Meanwhile, assemble the tamales. Take one husk, and with the waxy part of the husk facing up, add ¼ cup (55 g) of the blue corn dough to the middle of the husk. Form the dough into a 3 by 1-inch (8 by 2.5 cm) rectangle. Roll the husks lengthwise so that the dough is fully covered. Then fold in the top and bottom parts of the folded husks to the center. Tie each folded end with a strip of corn husk.

8. Add the wrapped tamales to the boiling water and let boil for 30 minutes, covered, until firm.

9. Let the tamales cool for at least 10 minutes before eating. Serve alone or with berry compote drizzled on top.

Daadlánígíí
DRINKS

Some of the best conversations are had over a
delicious beverage. And, whenever I feel homesick,
a cup of Navajo tea is always the best cure. It is
custom in Navajo culture to greet and send off
guests with drinks, typically a delicious hot coffee.
In this section, I share some of my favorite drinks.

Ch'il Ahwééh
Navajo Tea

Navajo tea is an Indigenous wild tea that is commonly called greenthread tea. In the Navajo language we call it ch'il ahwééh, or simply just dééh. It can be found in the Southwest, and is also consumed by other tribes, like the Hopi, Pueblo, and Apache. It can be served hot or cold. It has a mildly earthy and grassy flavor, and the scent reminds me of home. Some of my favorite memories growing up were when shimá would brew Navajo tea in her white enamelware kettle.

This recipe calls for a bundle of Navajo tea, which is sold preassembled and can be found at local flea markets, trading posts on the Navajo reservation, and sometimes online.

Note: You can make at least two to three batches of Navajo tea with one bundle. After serving, I will brew up another batch to have for second servings. Then I'll brew another batch and chill it to make iced tea or use it in Strawberry Navajo Iced Tea (page 150).

Yield: 4 servings	Prep time: 2 minutes	Cook time: 10 minutes
1 bundle (about 1 ounce, or 28 g) Navajo tea Honey, sugar, and/or sweetener of your choice, for serving	**1.** In a medium saucepan, combine the tea and 6 cups (1.4 L) of water. Bring to a boil over medium-high heat and let boil for 5 to 8 minutes. **2.** Pour the tea through a fine-mesh strainer. **3.** Ladle into mugs and serve with honey.	

Dahwoozh Déého hk'azí
Strawberry Navajo Iced Tea

This is a variation on traditional Navajo tea, or ch'il ahwééh. Iced Navajo tea is commonly served during the summer months. The strawberry puree gives the tea some fun flavor and brightness. This recipe also works well with watermelon, peaches, and blueberries.

Yield: 4 servings	Prep time: 20 minutes	Cook time: 15 minutes

1 cup (165 g) diced (¼ inch, or 6 mm) strawberries

2 tablespoons sugar

4 cups (960 ml) chilled Navajo Tea (page 149)

1 to 2 cups (217 to 435 g) ice cubes

1. In a small saucepan, add the strawberries, sugar, and ½ cup (120 ml) water and stir until the sugar is dissolved.

2. Bring the mixture to a boil over medium-high heat and let it boil for 5 minutes. Reduce the heat to medium-low and cook for 10 minutes, or until the liquid has reduced to a quarter of the original volume. Remove the mixture from the heat and let it cool for 15 minutes.

3. Place the strawberry mixture in a blender or food processor and blend on high for 1 to 2 minutes, until the mixture is smooth.

4. Pass the strawberry puree through a strainer into a large pitcher to remove the seeds. Then add the Navajo tea and mix until combined.

5. Pour the tea into glasses over ice and serve immediately.

Abe' Boba Dééhk'azí

Navajo Boba Milk Tea

Boba milk tea is a popular Taiwanese tea drink that combines boba (tapioca pearls) with black or green tea and milk. Boba tea has gained popularity on the Navajo Nation in the last few years, and you will find Navajo tea versions being sold at local flea markets and public events. My favorite version is Navajo tea, boba, honey, and oat milk. Variations of this recipe include using the Strawberry Navajo Iced Tea (page 150) and adding strawberry-flavored popping boba.

Yield: 4 servings	Prep time: 30 minutes	Cook time: 15 minutes

1 cup (150 g) uncooked boba/black tapioca pearls

2 teaspoons honey

2 to 3 cups (435 to 652 g) ice

4 cups (960 ml) Navajo Tea (page 149), chilled

1 cup (240 ml) oat milk or other milk of choice

1. Prepare the boba: In a medium saucepan, bring 4 cups (960 ml) of water to a boil over medium-high heat. Add the tapioca pearls and let boil for 5 to 8 minutes, until the boba is soft but slightly firm. Drain the boba in a mesh strainer and rinse with cold water for 1 to 2 minutes, until cooled.

2. Transfer the boba to a small bowl. Add the honey and stir until all the boba is coated.

3. To each cup, add ¼ cup (38 g) of boba, ½ cup (108 g) of ice, and 1 cup (240 ml) of Navajo tea. Top with ¼ cup (60 ml) of oat milk.

4. Serve cold with boba straws.

Chiiłchin Dééhk'azí

Sumac Berry Tea

Sumac berry tea, or chiiłchin dééhk'azí, is a traditional Navajo fruit tea that uses the dried and ground berries of the sumac bush (see page 17). It is also a popular Indigenous tea. The Navajo variety is the three-leaf sumac (*Rhus trilobata* Nutt.) that is common to New Mexico and Arizona. One of the distinguishing flavors of the tea is its natural lemony, tart flavor. It can be served hot or cold.

Yield: 4 servings	Prep time: 2 minutes	Cook time: 10 minutes
2 tablespoons ground sumac berries Honey, sugar, and/or sweetener of your choice, for serving	**1.** In a medium saucepan, combine the ground sumac berries and 4 cups (960 ml) of water and stir to combine. **2.** Bring the mixture to a boil over medium-high heat and let boil for about 10 minutes, or until the tea is a light red color. **3.** Pour the tea through a fine-mesh strainer. **4.** Ladle into mugs and serve with honey.	

Chiiłchin Tółtólí Dééhk'azí
Sumac Berry Spritzer

This sumac berry spritzer, or chiiłchin sparkler, is a fun recipe that incorporates the traditional flavors of ground sumac berries (see page 17) with raspberries and seltzer to create a fruity and tart drink. It is not a traditional recipe, but it is a fun way to combine modern flavors. This is the perfect drink for a summer cookout or an afternoon refresher. For a sweeter and fizzier flavor, use club soda instead.

Yield: 4 servings	Prep time: 10 minutes

1 cup (125 g) fresh raspberries

¼ cup (50 g) sugar

1 teaspoon ground sumac berries

3 cups (720 ml) seltzer or sparkling mineral water

1 to 2 cups (217 to 435 g) ice

1. Add the raspberries and sugar to a large pitcher and mix lightly with a wooden spoon. Then, muddle the raspberries, sugar, and ground sumac berries together until the raspberries are broken down into a puree.

2. Pour in the seltzer. Mix until the puree is fully incorporated.

3. Pour into cups with ice and serve immediately.

Neeshch'íí' Abe' Latte
Piñon Latte

Coffee is a staple in Navajo cuisine, and you will find it at almost every meal. Depending on the region of the Navajo Nation, coffee is either called gohwééh or ahwééh. (I grew up in the northern region, so I call it ahwééh.) This recipe combines Piñon Nut Butter (page 120), oat milk, coffee, and maple syrup. It is the perfect morning treat that highlights the toasted flavor of pine nuts, or piñons (if they are harvested from New Mexico), which are a coveted treat in Navajo cuisine. This recipe can also be served cold over ice.

Yield: 2 servings	Prep time: 10 minutes

2 tablespoons Piñon Nut Butter (page 120)

½ cup (120 ml) oat milk or other milk of your choice

4 shots (120 ml) brewed espresso, or 2 cups (480 ml) hot brewed coffee

2 teaspoons maple syrup

1. In a blender, add the piñon nut butter, oat milk, espresso, and maple syrup. Blend on high for 1 to 2 minutes, until smooth and frothy.

2. Pour into mugs and serve immediately.

Ahwééh dóó Ts'áálbáí
Navajo Coffee/Corn Creamer

Traditionally, corn creamer is made from parched Navajo white corn. This recipe is a modern take. Rather than parching the corn, this recipe calls for neeshjízhii, which is dried steam corn that is ground into a fine meal and toasted. The resulting meal can be added to coffee like a creamer. The creamer will settle to the bottom of the cup, so stir occasionally while drinking. You can purchase dried steam corn at local flea markets and trading posts on the Navajo Nation. It is also sold online by Navajo farmers.

Yield: 12 servings	Prep time: 15 minutes	Cook time: 5 minutes

¼ cup (50 g) dried steam corn (neeshjízhii)

1 cup (240 ml) brewed coffee

Honey, sugar, and/or sweetener of your choice, for serving

1. Place the dried steam corn in a coffee grinder and blend on high for 2 minutes, or until the corn forms into a fine meal. With a small metal sifter, sift the cornmeal into a medium bowl and discard any large corn sediments left in the sifter. Sift the cornmeal once more.

2. Grind the sifted cornmeal in the coffee grinder one more time, blending on high for 1 minute. Sift the cornmeal into the bowl once more, discarding any large corn sediments.

3. Transfer the ground cornmeal to a small pan and toast it over medium heat for 5 to 8 minutes, stirring continuously with a wooden spoon, until it starts to turn a darker shade of yellow. Remove from the heat and let cool for 5 minutes. Once it is cool, store the corn creamer in a small airtight jar in a cool, dark pantry for about 6 months.

4. Add 1 to 2 teaspoons of the corn creamer to a mug, pour in the brewed coffee, and mix. Serve with honey and enjoy.

Dibé Bits'in Atoo'
Mutton Bone Broth

In the typical Navajo diet, sheep are the main source of meat. All parts of the sheep are used. The bones, for example, are usually added to soups for a richer flavor. Mutton broth as a drink is not common to traditional Navajo cuisine, but bone broths have become quite popular in modern American cuisine, as they are high in collagen and protein. This recipe is a fusion of traditional and modern cooking methods to make a healthy drink. This quick broth can be made in about 30 minutes, and you can use leftover mutton/lamb bones; however, if you have time, you can make a larger batch and simmer the broth longer to extract more of the health benefits from the bones. Alternatively, you can use this broth as a base for soups and stews.

Yield: 4 cups	Prep time: 5 minutes	Cook time: 30 minutes

1 pound (455 g) roasted mutton bones

1 teaspoon apple cider vinegar

1. Place the bones in a large colander and rinse them under cold water for 1 to 2 minutes.

2. In a medium pot, combine the bones, 5 cups (1.2 L) of cold water, and the vinegar. Bring the mixture to a boil over medium-high heat, then let boil for 10 minutes.

3. Reduce the heat to a low simmer and let the bones simmer for 20 minutes, until the broth has reduced to 75 percent of its initial volume and the color is light yellow.

4. Strain into mugs and serve immediately.

Appendix

Navajo- and Native American–Owned Food Resources

As mentioned in the section on pantry staples (page 15), here is a list of Navajo and Native American–owned businesses that sell some of the specialty items I use in my recipes. Please note that some of these items, like Navajo dried steam corn, are sold seasonally and may only be available during certain times of the year. By supporting these businesses, you are not only supporting small business but also authentic American Indian foods.

Beesézį
Location: Shiprock, New Mexico
Website: www.beesezi.com
Products sold: Juniper ash, Navajo dried steam corn, roasted cornmeal (blue, white, and yellow)

Ben Farms
Location: Shiprock, New Mexico
Website: www.benfarms.com
Products sold: Navajo dried steam corn

Bidii Baby Foods LLC
Location: Shiprock, New Mexico
Website: www.bidiibabyfoods.org
Instagram: @bidiibabyfoods
Products sold: Navajo dried steam corn

Blue Corn Custom Designs
Location: Queen Creek, Arizona
Website: www.bccdofficial.com
Instagram: @BlueCornCustomDesigns
Products sold: Blue cornmeal, Navajo tea, juniper ash

Bow & Arrow Brand
Location: Towaoc, Colorado
Website: www.bowandarrowbrand.com
Products sold: Cornmeal (blue, white, and yellow)

Indian Pueblo Store
Location: Albuquerque, NM
Website: www.indianpueblostore.com
Products sold: Blue cornmeal, red chile powder

Indigenous Food Lab Market
Location: Minneapolis, Minnesota
Website: iflmarket.square.site
Products sold: Blue cornmeal, tepary beans, olive oil, maple syrup, honey

Navajo Pride by Navajo Agriculture Products Industry
Location: Farmington, New Mexico
Website: napi.navajopride.com
Products sold: Russet potatoes, pinto beans, roasted cornmeal (blue, white, and yellow), juniper ash, Navajo tea, ground sumac berries

Ramona Farms
Location: Sacaton, Arizona
Website: store.ramonafarms.com
Instagram: @teparybeans
Products sold: Blue cornmeal, tepary beans

Séka Hills
Location: Brooks, California
Website: www.sekahills.com
Instagram: @sekahills
Products sold: Olive oil, honey

Shima of Navajoland
Location: Fort Defiance, Arizona
Website: shimaofnavajoland.com
Products sold: Roasted blue cornmeal, juniper ash, honey

Sweetgrass Trading
Location: Winnebago, Nebraska
Website: sweetgrasstradingco.com
Instagram: @sweetgrasstradingco
Products sold: Tepary beans, blue cornmeal, maple syrup, honey

The Fancy Navajo
Location: Phoenix, Arizona
Website: TheFancyNavajo.com
Instagram: @TheFancyNavajo
Products sold: Roasted blue cornmeal

Tocabe Indigenous Marketplace
Location: Denver, Colorado
Website: shoptocabe.com
Instagram: @tocabe
Products sold: Cornmeal (blue, white, yellow), pinto beans, tepary beans, olive oil, juniper ash, maple syrup, honey

Other Food Resources

Bueno Foods

Location: Albuquerque, New Mexico

Website: buenofoods.com

Instagram: @buenofoods

Products sold: New Mexico red chile powder, New Mexico dried red chile pods, frozen green chiles

Hatch Chile Store

Location: Hatch, New Mexico

Website: www.hatch-green-chile.com

Instagram: @hatchgreenchile

Products sold: Roasted Hatch green chiles (fresh and frozen), New Mexico dried red chile pods, red chile powder, pinto beans

Los Chileros

Location: Albuquerque, New Mexico

Website: www.loschileros.com

Instagram: @loschileros

Products sold: New Mexico red chile powder, New Mexico dried red chile pods, roasted blue cornmeal, corn husks

The Original Sweetmeat

Location: Waterflow, New Mexico

Products sold: Fresh mutton and lamb, roasted cornmeal (blue, white, and yellow), juniper ash, Navajo steamed dried corn

T&R Market

Location: Gallup, New Mexico

Website: www.t-rmarket.com

Products sold: Fresh mutton and lamb, Hatch green chiles, roasted blue cornmeal

Valley Trading Post

Location: Waterflow, New Mexico

Products sold: Fresh mutton and lamb, roasted cornmeal (blue, white, and yellow), juniper ash, Navajo steamed dried corn, ground sumac berries, Navajo tea, corn husks

Traditional Navajo Cooking Tools and Measurements

When it comes to traditional Navajo cooking tools, I frequently use my Navajo stirring sticks, grinding stone, and cast-iron campfire grill as a way to carry my traditional teaching into the modern world. Whenever I use these tools, I feel more connected to my Navajo heritage and think about all the memories and stories tied to them.

Measurements

When it comes to traditional Navajo cooking, measuring cups and spoons are not common. As mentioned in my introduction (page 7), this was one of the most fascinating things to me as a child. Shimá and shimásání would make every meal with no standardized measurements, especially when it came to making traditional Navajo foods. Instead, they would rely on the cups of their hands and the pinches of their fingers to measure out ingredients. These measurements were often tricky when I was a child, because at the time my hands were a lot smaller than my mom's. As I get older, I am finding that I am getting more comfortable using these traditional measurements as I make traditional recipes more frequently. However, measuring spoons and cups are still part of my modern Navajo kitchen, especially when it comes to more advanced baking recipes.

When I started writing out shimá's recipes, I began to realize how close these hand measurements are to standardized measuring tools. For instance, below are some traditional measurements and their equivalents. But please keep in mind that these may vary depending on hand sizes.

1 pinch (thumb and finger) = ⅛ teaspoon

Small center of palm cupped hand scoop = 1 teaspoon

1 full cupped hand scoop = ½ cup (115 g)

Index finger (first knuckle to middle knuckle) = 1 inch (2.5 cm)

Navajo Grinding Stone

Navajo grinding stones are traditional tools to grind corn into cornmeal used in cooking and ceremonies. It consists of two parts: the bottom, or tsédaashjéé', and the top stone, or tsédaasch'iní. The bottom stone is a large rectangular stone and the top stone is a smaller, handheld rectangular-shaped stone. Together they create a horizontal grinder that is used in a kneeling position. Grinding stones are typically made from tsé dildo'i, or hard rock. Grinding stones can range in size from as large as 16 inches (41 cm) by 12 inches (30 cm) or bigger, to smaller sizes of 5 inches (13 cm) by 7 inches (18 cm). I have a smaller grinding stone in my kitchen that I use to quickly grind cornmeal. Larger grinding stones are usually passed down from generation to generation. In modern times, a metal hand-crank grain grinder is used instead of a grinding stone when grinding large batches of cornmeal.

Shimásání taught me how to grind corn on a large grinding stone that had been in our family for generations at my kinaaldá. I couldn't believe how much work went into grinding corn into a fine meal. All my cousins and aunties took turns helping me. I remember being amazed about how these tools connected everyone as we all sat in the hogan (a traditional Navajo home) taking turns grinding corn, sharing stories and feeling closer to each other.

Cast-Iron Campfire Grill

Traditional Navajo foods are cooked outside on an open fire. My family didn't really have a traditional American-style grill growing up; rather, we had a homemade grill made of cinderblocks and a large metal grate in our backyard. We used this a lot in the summer and fall months to make delicious meals like roast mutton, roast green chiles, tortillas, and fry bread. Having an outside grill was important because, like our kitchen, it brought us all together. Shimásání usually cooked directly on the ground and would add a grill over the open fire to make juniper ash and cook other traditional meals. When I moved away, my husband and I made sure we had a small cast-iron campfire grill that we use to make Fry Bread (page 34), roast mutton, and Navajo Tortillas (page 33). Tortillas made on an outdoor grill are so delicious! The added char and crisp of the tortilla, along with freshly roasted mutton and green chile, makes for the perfect summer meal.

Navajo Stirring Sticks

Navajo stirring sticks, or ádístsiin, are traditional Navajo cooking tools used to mix traditional Navajo foods like cornmeal mushes, and can also be used to make 'alkaad. These sticks can range from 12 to 36 inches (30 to 91 cm) long and are made from greasewood, a bush that is common on the Navajo Nation. Depending on who makes the ádítsiin, there are five to seven sticks symbolizing different Navajo teachings that are tied together with a string. One common teaching is that Navajo stirring sticks are protection tools for Navajo women as a way to ward off hunger for their families. You will often find a set of Navajo stirring sticks hung on the kitchen wall or above the doorways of Navajo homes for that reason. These are commonly gifted during a kinaaldá or wedding, but may also be purchased for any occasion. In my personal kitchen, I frequently use my stirring sticks in place of a whisk.

As a young child I remember seeing shimá's set of stirring sticks hanging on the wall above our kitchen table and asking her what they were for. She said they were her protection tools and that by having them in our home, it would ward off hunger and poverty and that one day I would have a set of my own. I didn't see her use these tools until my kinaaldá. It was the first time I saw her take down her sticks from the wall, which she used to help me stir the large batches

of cornmeal for the ceremony. Shimá didn't have a kinaaldá growing up and as her only daughter, this was a celebration we talked about in the years leading up to my ceremony. She had eagerly set aside these stirring sticks in preparation for this event. I received my first set of Navajo stirring sticks then too.

Cameron, Arizona

Sample Meal Plans

One of my goals with this cookbook is to inspire others to incorporate more Navajo and Indigenous foods into their diets. Below are sample meal plans that can be used to incorporate the recipes shared in this cookbook into your everyday lifestyle.

The Modern Navajo Weekly Meal Plan

Sunday
Breakfast: Piñon Lattes (page 158), Blue Corn Pancakes (page 61) with Berry Compote (page 123) and bacon
Lunch: Turkey Sandwich with Three Sisters Pasta Salad (page 115)
Dinner: Navajo Tacos (page 93)
Dessert: Blue Corn Cupcakes (page 128)

Monday
Breakfast: Blue Corn Mush Breakfast Fruit Bowl (page 49)
Lunch: Leftover Chili Beans (page 74) from Navajo Tacos with saltine crackers
Dinner: Navajo Burgers (page 94) with leftover Three Sisters Pasta Salad

Tuesday
Breakfast: Corn Granola (page 58) with yogurt
Lunch: Savory Blue Corn Mush Bowl (page 83)
Dinner: Navajo Pizza (page 104) using leftover tortillas from Navajo Burgers

Wednesday
Breakfast: Rice Pudding with Cranberries (page 57)
Lunch: Three Sisters Stew (page 78)
Dinner: Potatoes and Ground Beef Bowl (page 97) with Biscuits (page 37)

Thursday
Breakfast: Leftover Biscuits with Piñon Nut Butter (page 120)
Lunch: Squash, Corn, and Green Chile Bowl (page 98)
Dinner: Lamb Meatballs (page 103) with Sumac Berry Jam (page 119)

Friday
Breakfast: Sumac Berry Pudding (page 50)
Lunch: Leftover Lamb Meatballs with Sumac Berry Jam
Dinner: Steam Corn Stew (page 73)

Saturday
Breakfast: SPAM/Canned Meat Breakfast Burrito (page 54)
Lunch: Leftover Steam Corn Stew
Dinner: Green Chile Stew (page 77) with Blue Corn Bread (page 41)

Seasonal Meal Plans

This section of meal plans has been split into seasons. Some of the ingredients needed to make these dishes are only available during certain times of the year, so the meal plans shared below can act as a guide to show which dishes are commonly made during each season. However, since I tend to stock up on these items throughout the year, these dishes can be made year-round if you plan accordingly.

Spring Meal Plans

Breads
Navajo Tortillas (page 33)
Fry Bread (page 34)
Biscuits (page 37)
Blue Corn Patties (page 38)
Blue Corn Flour Tortillas (page 45)

Summer Meal Plans

Navajo Coffee/Corn Creamer (page 161)
Mutton Bone Broth (page 162)

The Fancy Navajo Tea Party

Perfect for bridal showers, Mother's Day, or birthdays for all ages, let this meal plan give you some inspiration for anytime you want to feel a bit more *fancy*.

Breads
Blue Corn Patties (page 38)
Kneel Down Bread (page 42)
Biscuits with Sumac Berry Jam (page 119)
White Corn Scones with Apricots (page 65)

Main Dishes
Blue Corn Quiche (page 53)
Sumac Berry Fruit Salad (page 116)

Desserts
Blue Corn Cupcakes (page 128)
Sumac Berry Sugar Cookies (page 135)
Blue Corn Strawberry Shortcakes (page 140)
Navajo Sweet Corn Cake (page 132)

Drinks
Navajo Tea (page 149)
Sumac Berry Tea (page 154)

The Navajo Feast

I often talk about family gatherings, and this is a sample meal plan of what can be served at large celebrations like birthday parties, graduations, anniversaries, or holidays. These include traditional staples and modern dishes that are easy to make for large gatherings and will wow your guests.

Breads
Navajo Tortillas (page 33)
Fry Bread (page 34)

Blue Corn Bread (page 41)

Soups & Stews
Mutton and Vegetable Stew (page 69)
Green Chile Stew (page 77)
Steam Corn Stew (page 73)
Chili Beans (page 74)

Main Dishes
Traditional Mutton Ribs (page 89)
Lamb Sandwich (page 90)
Navajo Burger (page 94)
Navajo Tacos (page 93)

Sides
Blue Corn Bread Stuffing (page 111)
Sumac Berry Pudding (page 50)
Three Sisters Pasta Salad (page 115)
Sumac Berry Fruit Salad (page 116)
Corn Salsa (page 124)
Blue Corn Mush Breakfast Fruit Bowl (page 49)
Savory Blue Corn Mush Bowl (page 83)

Desserts
Blue Corn Cupcakes (page 128)
Blue Corn Strawberry Shortcakes (page 140)
Piccadilly (page 131)
Navajo Sweet Corn Cake (page 132)
Sumac Berry Sugar Cookies (page 135)

Drinks
Navajo Tea (page 149)
Sumac Berry Tea (page 154)
Strawberry Navajo Iced Tea (page 150)
Sumac Berry Spritzer (page 157)

A Glossary of Navajo Words

'abe' bee neezmasí – blue corn pancakes

'alkaad /'alkaan – sweet corn cake

abe' boba dééhk'azí – boba milk tea

abínígo daadánígíí – breakfast

'ach'ii' – sheep intestines wrapped around the sheep's fat or colon

ádístsiin – stirring sticks

ahwééh – coffee

ahwééh dóó ts'áałbáí – coffee with corn creamer

alóós cranberry bee naashgizhkání – rice pudding with cranberries

aneest'e' ałtaas'éí chiiłchin bitoo' bik'isziidí – sumac berry fruit salad

atoo' ádaat'éhígíí – soups or stews

atoo' azeedích'ííłt'izhí bił – green chile stew

atsį' SPAM/yadiizíní atsį' náneeskadí bił yisdisí – SPAM/canned meat breakfast burrito

atsį' yik'ą́ náneeskadí bił ałch'į' át'éhí – burger

ayoo' shił łikan – "It tastes really good to me."

azeedích'ííłchí'í dibé bitsį' ak'ah bii' yizaazgo dóó tó ałchx'į́dígo bee shibéezhí – braised red chile mutton stew

bááh danilínígíí – breads

bááh dootł'izhi – blue corn patties; blue corn bread

bááh nímazí – biscuits

bił asdisí ádaat'éhígíí – sandwiches

ch'il ahwééh – Navajo tea (see dééh)

chiiłchin bááh dá'áka'í – sumac berry cookies

chiiłchin dééhk'azí – sumac berry tea

chiiłchin jelii – sumac berry jam

chiiłchin naadą́ą' ak'áán bee naashgizhkání – sumac berry pudding

chiiłchin tółtólí dééhk'azí – sumac berry spritzer

chiiłchin yogurt tiní – sumac and strawberry Greek yogurt ice pops

daadlánígíí – drinks

dah díníilghaazh – fry bread

dah díníilghaazh bikáá' ashjaa'í – Navajo taco

dahistin – ice cream

dahwoozh dééhk'azí – strawberry iced tea

dahwoozh dóó blueberries bitoo'kání – berry compote

dééh – Navajo tea (see ch'il ahwééh)

dibé bits'in atoo' – mutton bone broth

dibé bitsį' 'atoo' – mutton and vegetable stew

dibé bitsį' – roasted mutton ribs

dibé yázhí bitsį' lees'áán bił yisdisí – lamb sandwich

dibé yázhí bitsį' naadą́ą' yik'ą́ bił meatballs ályaaí – lamb meatballs with cornmeal

dił'oodi – apricots

Diné – the Navajo people

Diyin Diné'é – the holy people

gad bee łeeshch'iih – juniper ash

gohwééh – coffee

hogan – a traditional Navajo home

hózho - harmony and balance

íyisí daadą́ą́go daabiłígíí – sides

íyisí daadánígíí – main dishes

k'íneeshbízhii 'atoo' – dumpling stew

kinaaldá – a coming of age ceremony celebrating Navajo womanhood that occurs when a Navajo girl has her first period

Kinyaa'áanii - Towering House Clan

likání ádaat'éhígíí – desserts

naa'ołí azeedích'íí'- chili beans

naa'ołí azeedích'íí' naadą́ą́' báahkáa'í – chili bean cornmeal casserole

naadą́ą́'áłtsóí sit'é azeedích'íí' bił tanaashgiizhí – corn salsa

naadą́ą́'élgai áłtsé nit'į́į́h bááhkání – white corn scones with apricots

naadą́ą́'éłgai tamale atsį' yik'ą́ dóó azeedích'ííłchí'í bił – tamales

naadą́ą́' dootł'izh taa'niil – blue corn mush

naadą́ą́' ak'áán granola – corn granola

naadą́ą́' dootł'izhí bááhkání yázhí – blue corn cupcakes

naadą́ą́' dootł'izhí báahtaas'éí – blue corn bread stuffing

naadą́ą́' dootł'izhí dahwoozh bááhłkání – blue corn strawberry shortcake

naadą́ą́' dootł'izhí naayízí waffle – blue corn pumpkin waffles

naadą́ą́' dootł'izhí náneeskaadí – blue corn flour tortillas

naadą́ą́' dootł'izhí quiche – blue corn quiche

naadą́ą́' dootł'izhí tamaliiłkání – sweet blue corn tamales

naayízí – pumpkin

naayízí bááh dá'áka'í – maple pumpkin cookies

naayízí, naadą́ą́' dóó azeedích'íí' dootł'izhí ak'ah áłchx'į́į́ dígo bee sit'éhi – squash, corn, and green chile bowl

náneeskaadí – tortillas

náneeskadí téél atsį' dóó saucełchí'í bił – tortilla pizza

neeshch'íí' abe' latte – piñon latte

neeshchx'íí' mandigíiya – piñon nut butter

neeshjį́zhii 'atoo' – steam corn stew

neeshjį́zhii' – dried steam corn

nímasii dóó atsį' yik'ą̨st'éhi – potatoes and ground beef bowl

nímasii dóó atsį' spam atoo' – potato and SPAM soup

nitsidigo'í – kneel down bread

shich'é'é – daughter

shik'éí – family

shimá – mom

shimásání – maternal grandmother

shínaaí – older brother

shizhé'é – dad

Tábaaha - Waters Edge Clan

Ta'neeszahnii – the Tangle Clan

táá' ałdeezhí atoo' – three sisters stew

táá' ałdeezhí ch'il ałtaas'éí – three sisters pasta salad

tin ta'neesk'áník'ǫzhí chiiłchin yik'ání bił – piccadilly

Tót'sohn'nii – Big Water Clan

tsé dildo'I – hard rock (referring to a Navajo grinding stone)

tsédaasch'iní – the top stone of the Navajo grinding stone

tsédaashjéé' – the bottom stone of the Navajo grinding stone

References

Diné Policy Institute. *Diné Food Sovereignty: A Report of the Navajo Nation Food System and the Case to Rebuild a Self-Sufficient System for the Diné People.* Published April 2014. www.dinecollege.edu/wp-content/uploads/2018/04/dpi-food-sovereignty-report.pdf.

Frisbie, Charlotte. *Food Sovereignty the Navajo Way: Cooking with Tall Woman.* Albuquerque: University of New Mexico Press, 2018.

Kopp, Jody. "Crosscultural Contacts: Changes in the Diet and Nutrition of the Navajo Indians." *American Indian Culture and Research Journal.* 10:4 (1986): 1–30. nec.navajo-nsn.gov/Portals/0/NN%20Research/General%20Navajo%20Health/1986_%20Crosscultural%20Contacts-Changes%20in%20the%20diet%20and%20nutrition%20of%20the%20Navajo%20Indians.pdf.

Mayes, Vernon, and Barbara Bayless Lacy. *Nanise', A Navajo Herbal: One Hundred Plants from the Navajo Reservation.* Chandler, AZ: Five Star Publications, Inc., 2012

Morales, Laurel. "To Get Calcium, Navajos Burn Juniper Branches to Eat the Ash." National Public Radio (NPR). Published August 21, 2017. www.npr.org/sections/thesalt/2017/08/21/544191316/to-get-calcium-navajos-burn-juniper-branches-to-eat-the-ash.

Parsons Yazzie, Evangeline, and Margaret Speas. *Diné Bizaad Bínáhoo'aah: Rediscovering the Navajo Language.* Flagstaff, AZ: Salin Bookshelf, Inc., 2007.

Shiprock, New Mexico

Index

Horseshoe Bend, Arizona

Acknowledgments

There are so many people that made this cookbook possible. This was an absolute dream come true and without my supporters of *The Fancy Navajo*, this wouldn't have come about. I appreciate all of your support and encouragement throughout the years. Thank you for taking the time out of your day to read my blog. Thank you to all the friends and businesses that I found through social media!

Thank you to my family for their continuous teachings throughout my lifetime. Thank you to my mom, dad, Chet, and my eldest brother for the endless talks we had about Navajo foods and cooking. Thank you for taking time to share your personal stories and going out of your way to make sure all my questions were answered. Thank you to shimá for always having patience with me in the kitchen and for encouraging me to write down the recipes. Thank you to my late shimásání for all her traditional teachings and for always encouraging me to learn.

To my husband, thank you for all your patience and kindness throughout this process. Your encouragement helped me push through. You were the best taste tester and I appreciated all the love and support. Thank you for always believing in my dreams and helping to make them come true. To my daughter, this book is for you. It's our family cookbook and I hope you continue to build upon it. Always keep learning! Ayóó ánííshní! (I love you!)

Thank you so much to the wonderful people at Quarto and all their help in getting this project started. To Rage, thank you for reaching out and making me feel comfortable throughout this process. To my editor, Elizabeth, thank you for helping my stories come alive and for all the edits to make this a masterpiece. I appreciate all your attention to detail. To the design team, Laura and Marisa, thank you for making this book look absolutely gorgeous!!

I'd also like to thank my dear friend Jennifer Hubbell, whom I graciously met on Instagram when I first started. Not only do I call her my Instagram bestie, but she truly is someone I love and admire. Thank you tremendously for all your teachings about photography and editing. I am so glad we met and your work continuously inspires me. I am so happy you were able to help contribute some of your photos to this cookbook.

A huge thank you to Irene Silentman for helping with the Navajo recipe title translations and for the Navajo subtitle of this book. Your knowledge of the oral and written Navajo language was immensely helpful and I learned a lot along the way. I am excited to use these recipe translations more!!

Also THANK YOU for making this book a part of your collection! A big ahéhee' (thank you)!

About the Author

Alana Yazzie is the creator of *The Fancy Navajo*, a lifestyle and food blog started in 2014 that follows Alana's life as a contemporary Diné/Navajo woman living in Phoenix, Arizona. Originally from northwest New Mexico, Alana inspires others to embrace their culture, wherever they live, by sharing lifestyle content, such as recipes, fashion, and gardening, infused with her Navajo heritage. Alana's greatest passion is developing innovative and approachable recipes that use Indigenous and southwestern ingredients. Through *The Fancy Navajo*, she enjoys capturing her Navajo lifestyle in modern and bright settings to showcase the continued presence and thriving of Indigenous Peoples. Alana can be found on Instagram @TheFancyNavajo, on Facebook @TheFancyNavajoBlog, and on her website, TheFancyNavajo.com.

© 2024 by Quarto Publishing Group USA Inc.
Text and Photography © 2024 by Alana Yazzie

First published in 2024 by Wellfleet Press,
an imprint of The Quarto Group,
142 West 36th Street, 4th Floor,
New York, NY 10018, USA
(212) 779-4972
www.Quarto.com

All rights reserved. No part of this book may be reproduced in any form without written permission of the copyright owners. All images in this book have been reproduced with the knowledge and prior consent of the artists concerned, and no responsibility is accepted by producer, publisher, or printer for any infringement of copyright or otherwise, arising from the contents of this publication. Every effort has been made to ensure that credits accurately comply with information supplied. We apologize for any inaccuracies that may have occurred and will resolve inaccurate or missing information in a subsequent reprinting of the book.

Wellfleet Press titles are also available at discount for retail, wholesale, promotional, and bulk purchase. For details, contact the Special Sales Manager by email at specialsales@quarto.com or by mail at The Quarto Group, Attn: Special Sales Manager, 100 Cummings Center Suite 265D, Beverly, MA 01915 USA.

10 9 8 7 6 5 4 3 2 1

ISBN: 978-1-57715-467-9

Digital edition published in 2024
eISBN: 978-0-7603-9220-1

Library of Congress Cataloging-in-Publication Data

Names: Yazzie, Alana, author.
Title: The modern Navajo kitchen : homestyle recipes that celebrate the
  flavors and traditions of the Diné = Diné bibee ó'ool'įįł
  bits'ą́ą́dóó bóhoneed'į́igo hooghan góne' ádaal'į́igo
  daadánígíí / Alana Yazzie.
Description: New York, NY : Wellfleet Press, 2024. | Includes
  bibliographical references and index. | Summary: "The Modern Navajo
  Kitchen spotlights Navajo cuisine and culture with over 50 recipes"--
  Provided by publisher.
Identifiers: LCCN 2024011752 (print) | LCCN 2024011753 (ebook) | ISBN
  9781577154679 (hardcover) | ISBN 9780760392201 (ebook)
Subjects: LCSH: Navajo cooking. | Navajo Indians--Food. | Cooking,
  American--Southwestern style. | LCGFT: Cookbooks.
Classification: LCC E99.N3 Y39 2025 (print) | LCC E99.N3 (ebook) | DDC
  641.5929726--dc23/eng/20240320
LC record available at https://lccn.loc.gov/2024011752
LC ebook record available at https://lccn.loc.gov/2024011753

Group Publisher: Rage Kindelsperger
Creative Director: Laura Drew
Senior Art Director: Marisa Kwek
Editorial Director: Erin Canning
Managing Editor: Cara Donaldson
Editor: Elizabeth You
Cover and Interior Design: Laura Klynstra
Additional Photography: Jennifer Hubbell pages 10-11, 29, 170-171, 175, 189

Printed in China